I0706746

Cover designed by Angie with Fiverr
Edited by Kelcey Rockhold

Printed in the United States of America

First Printing: July 2017

ISBN: Paperback   9781983283932
        Kindle eBook   B07F5D13K4

FAMILY THE HARD WAY

Infertility, Autism, and Loss

Joyce Tejan

DEDICATION

I dedicate this book to all my family and friends who encouraged me to write this book. Their loving support and encouragement has spurred me on through the past ten years of thinking about finishing it, and finally completing it.

The other person to whom I would like to dedicate this book to is a woman whom I don't know at all. I would like to meet her someday, if possible. If she ever happens upon this book, she will know it's her, because there is one thing she has that no one else in the world has – a photo album with pictures of our precious son, Kevin.

SPECIAL PURPOSE

My deepest desire is to offer encouragement and hope to those whose lives have been touched by mental health struggles, infertility, or child loss. This is also for those who have faced similar circumstances and have not had a place for their voice to be heard.

INTRODUCTION

The reason I wrote this book, is to bring hope to others who have struggled with infertility, a child with autism or struggled to raise their child who has behavioral health issues or has experienced the loss of a child. I have thought of writing this story down for so long and have started and stopped numerous times throughout the past ten years. I finally finished what I started and want to share it with you now.

This book is an accumulation of a lifetime of experiences, events, adventures, some good and some bad. All of it has made me what I am today. I believe the best way to look at life is that everything is a blessing from God, and how you respond to life shapes you as a person. It's been more than any one person should have to handle, but somehow, I have just kept moving forward. I'm thankful that I can actually do this and share my story with those who need to hear it.

When I started writing this book, I never thought I'd have to include the loss of a second child, but that's the reality. My sincere hope is that someone reading this, can benefit from what my husband and I have endured, and find it inspiring and uplifting for themselves, a friend, or a family member.

Please note that some names have been changed to protect their privacy.

CONTENTS

PART ONE: SHADOW AND LIGHT

BLIND DATE

It was in July 1982, and I was selling Mary Kay Cosmetics. One day I called one of my clients for a re-order, and she said: "Oh, I gave your phone number to this guy I work with." I said, "What?" "Don't worry," she said. "He won't call you unless you want him to call." She proceeded to tell me that he was a computer technician, a very nice guy, and she thought we would get along great. I thought he sounded alright and told my friend that she could give him the "go ahead" to call me so that we could talk on the phone and decide if we wanted to meet each other. They both worked at the Jet Propulsion Laboratory (JPL) in Pasadena, California, and both of my parents had worked there many years ago as well. It brought a certain level of comfort to the conversation, which was nice.

I was waiting for his phone call and wondering if I would like the sound of his voice if I would like what he had to say. When he did call, we talked for a couple of hours. I don't even remember now what it was that we talked about, but whatever he said, it was good enough to set a date and time to meet! I had never been on a blind date. Would I like the way he looked? He sounded alright on the phone. Would we be attracted to each other? Would we enjoy each other's company? Would we have a fun or boring time? I guess time would tell.

It was an exciting time, preparing for our first date, and scary too. I had never been on a blind date before. I remember getting ready to meet him, and of course, I wanted to look and feel pretty and dress to impress. I wore a turquoise skirt and matching blouse with my opal earrings and necklace.

The doorbell rang. He was right on time, to the second. I opened the door to a handsome man leaning against the railing outside of my apartment. He looked nice. He was wearing black slacks and a nice dress shirt. His eyes were happy and kind. We went to dinner at Monaghan's Irish Pub in Pasadena, California. He had reserved a private booth for us, which had green velvet curtains draped on the sides of the booth, which drowned out some of the bar noise so we could talk and get to know each other. I had never been married before, but Paul had. He had been married previously for about two years before divorcing. I asked him a lot of questions about his relationship which allowed me to learn a lot about this new man I was now on a date with. Everything he said made me feel good. He hadn't scared me off yet! We had a nice evening and decided to keep dating so that we could really get to know each other.

Meeting potential dates wasn't our strong suit. We were both a little on the introverted side, and it was probably a good thing that a mutual friend of ours introduced us, or we would have never met. We weren't the type to stop at a bar after work to meet people. I guess you'd say we were both shy homebodies. Which is ok. You have to be who you are, and not try to be somebody else. What we did have in common was that we were both looking for someone special to have a relationship with.

As we dated, we went to each other's churches. His was quite different from mine. Paul's was a Lutheran church, and mine was a non-denominational church. He didn't like my type of church and said they were too wild and loud, like holy roller churches. I thought his was too rigid and boring.

I attended a private Christian school from first grade through twelfth grade and went to church every Sunday, and even more days than that. Paul was the son of a Lutheran pastor, and his grandfather had also been a Lutheran pastor for fifty years. Between his father and grandfather both retiring as Lutheran pastors, that's 100 years of Lutheran pastoring he was surrounded with. I think it wore him down by having to go to church all the time with his parents on Sunday, not to mention mid-week Bible studies and other church events. It was overwhelming to him, and I think that's why he doesn't really want to go to church today, which is o.k.! He was churched out.

At the time, we had talked about finding a church we both liked but never agreed on one. Eventually, we came to the conclusion that it's more important to have our faith and belief in God and who He is in one's personal life. If we found a church we both liked, then we would attend it. We were firm and secure in our belief in God and were comfortable with where we stood with God and Christianity. As for our parents, they thought we needed a church home to be happy and to go to heaven. We'll get to heaven, we aren't worried about that, and someday, maybe we will find a church that we both like.

We both enjoyed eating out, mostly at fast food restaurants, because they cost less, and then we could eat out more often. We also enjoyed going to the movies and spending time with each other. Paul preferred the science fiction movies, and I preferred romantic comedies. We went to both types and learned to eventually like each other's types of movies. We would go roller skating, and Paul was fantastic at roller skating. He worked as a floor guard in his teenage years and was involved in roller dance competitions. When he took me skating, he would swing me around the corners with a "Charisse" move that made me look like a great skater. He was the great skater, not me, but it was fast and a lot of fun. One day after skating, he asked me "Why do your lips taste so sweet?" What a come-on line, huh? I said it was Mary Kay Cosmetics strawberry lip gloss. He couldn't get enough of that.

We had been dating for only three months when it was my birthday. He went all-out on my special day. First, he gave me a beautiful gold Seiko watch, and then we went to dinner at the Bonaventure Hotel in Los Angeles. At the top of the hotel is a beautiful restaurant that turns slowly around the city showing the beautiful skyline. It's very romantic and expensive too. He said he had never spent that much on dinner before, but that I was worth it. It was a beautiful evening, and we were enjoying each other's company, and I think at that point was when we were truly falling in love.

I remember at Christmas time; we were visiting my mom's house in Escondido, California. Paul gave me a white rabbit fur coat. It was so warm and fuzzy, and I loved it! Nowadays it's considered taboo to wear a real fur coat, and looking back on it, I don't think I'd buy one again, but I enjoyed it a great deal at the time. He had another gift for me. It was a box of Cracker Jacks. I looked at the box and said "yum" and then tossed the box aside. Paul had to coax me to look at the Cracker Jacks a little closer.

He asked, "Did you check out the prize inside?" I hadn't, and he said that I better take another look because there was a nice prize inside the box. He had carefully and meticulously opened the box to take the "prize packet" out and replace the prize with a beautiful pair of teardrop pearl earrings. I loved them! He was so clever to hide them that way. It didn't look like he had tampered with the box at all.

Paul was able to do anything he set his mind to. He could figure anything out and fix anything that needed fixing. When we were dating, my Honda Civic needed some repairs. Whenever I turned right, smoke would come out of the steering column. So, I did everything I could to go left instead, so I didn't have too many right-hand turns to make; to get where I needed to go. Driving this way amazed him, and he offered to look at my car to see why it was smoking. He figured out the problem and repaired the wiring harness for the steering column, and my car worked perfectly again. No more smoking steering column. Paul sold Slick 50, an engine additive, and wanted my car to also have it, so it was protected. First, he changed the oil and then added the Slick 50. He told me later on in our courtship that when he was under the car changing the oil, he looked up at me and noticed I was wearing the cutest pair of red painter pants along with a gold ankle bracelet and wedged platform shoes. He said he couldn't believe his eyes and fell in love with me at that moment. I did look cute that day, I thought to myself, but it wasn't a girl trap like he thought it was. I was just "me." We talked about getting married before, and Paul would often say "let's run off to Las Vegas and get married." I'd just laugh it off and didn't take him too seriously. I didn't think he would want to marry me if he found out that I might have trouble having children. It was a worry I'd had since I was a teenager, due to irregular cycles and some other things that seemed "off." I felt like damaged goods, especially since we both wanted children. We were getting pretty serious, and I needed to tell him about the fact that I might not be able to get pregnant or might have difficulties. I told him everything that I knew up to that point, and he said that he loved me no matter what. If we couldn't have our own children, then we could adopt. He loved me for me, and I loved him for him. He was wonderful! I found a very good man. He said that after we were married, we could look into the reason why I might have a problem conceiving.

We had been dating for almost a year and a half, and he kept asking me casually to marry him. There wasn't a remarkable formal proposal like you see in the movies where the man gets on bended knee and pulls out a ring. I wasn't too sure how serious he really was, until one day he was a little more persistent, and I said I'd let him know. I thought about it, and not for too long (maybe a half a day), and I said "yes," I'd love to marry him.

We went to my mom and stepdad's house in Escondido, California to tell them the good news. They were very happy for us and knew it was just a matter of time before we decided to get engaged. My mom said, "When? Have you set a date yet?" We hadn't even thought about a date. It was already October and the holiday season was right around the corner. Either we get married soon, before the busy holiday time, or wait until after the first of the year. We didn't want to wait and decided on November 19, 1983. That meant a lot of planning, quickly.

With the wedding date set, it was only five weeks away with many things to get done in a short amount of time. We decided to get married in the Lutheran church where Paul was a member. It was a beautiful church, with the most amazing stained-glass windows and a beautiful pipe organ that sounded so majestic. Since I wasn't a member, the Pastor required us to go to marriage counseling to make sure we were ok to be married. We met with the pastor a couple of times in the evening after work.

My mom and I went shopping for my wedding dress. I had an idea of what I wanted from looking in the bridal magazines, but those dresses would take up to three months to have delivered, and they were very expensive, and we needed my dress in less than five weeks. We went shopping for something that looked close to it. We were driving around San Gabriel and noticed a small Hispanic wedding shop on the corner that sold wedding dresses. We decided to go into the shop. The owner happened to also be an incredible seamstress, and she made a lot of the dresses in her shop. I showed her a couple of pictures of what I wanted, and she said she could make it for me. I was so excited that she could make my dream wedding dress. She finished my dress in about three weeks, and it was beautiful!

I ordered a beautiful wedding cake with three tiers of chocolate cake with raspberry filling which was Paul's favorite. Our friends recommended a florist and photographer. I had a vision of carrying a beautiful bouquet flowers and having flowers and ribbons arranged down the church aisle. We both wanted a really good photographer. Those two things were the most important to us.

We were married five weeks after setting the date, on a Saturday, at the Trinity Lutheran church in San Gabriel. It was a beautiful ceremony with about eighty guests, and afterward, we had a reception in the church gathering hall. My mom, step-mom and a couple of neighbors made food for a buffet style lunch. It was simple but very beautiful.

When we were at the reception, my brother, Larry, asked Paul for the keys to our car. He said he was going to pull the car around to the front of the church and put some of our things in it. When we were ready to leave the church for our honeymoon, we went out to our car and found that my brother had filled the car with paper dots. There were dots everywhere! He worked in the printing department at JPL and had been saving boxes of dots for our wedding surprise, the kind of dots from hole punching paper. He filled the car, alright! It made a huge mess right in front of the church. My dad was mad because he had to pay someone to clean it up. Larry made a lasting impression. We were hoping to leave the church and be on the road for a short Las Vegas honeymoon getaway, but instead, we left the church and went directly to the carwash to try to clean up the dots. The employees there just snickered and did their best to vacuum up as many of the dots as they could. Several months later, we went on our official honeymoon cruise to the Bahamas, and Paul found "dots" in his suit pocket. We found dots everywhere for another couple of years whenever we cleaned out the car. We just laughed about it and told Larry we would pay him back someday. I think that subconsciously, he knows that we will get even at some point.

DREAMS SHATTERED

Wouldn't it be nice if life went just the way you wanted? Unfortunately, that's not reality. My dad always said hard times are called "life's learning experiences" and you grow stronger for what you endure. I didn't really like that saying and didn't feel it applied to me very much because I hadn't lived very much yet. I was in my early twenties, and at that time didn't know what was ahead for me on my road of life. It's probably a good thing I didn't know.

Paul and I had been married for about six months and were saving money to buy a house. We were hoping to be in a home of our own within a year or so. We also thought that it was time to find out what possible issues we might have in trying to conceive a baby. One day we met with my doctor, and he said he would need to perform a laparoscopy to find out for sure what was going on with me. We scheduled the procedure, and I was actually very excited to have surgery! Was I crazy? What was the heck the matter with me? Surgery could be risky, but I was never afraid to be operated on because I knew it was going to give me some answers, and it was something I knew I needed to go through. It was the beginning of being able to start our family together, or so I thought.

I remember my dad and stepmom were at the hospital that day, along with Paul, of course. The surgery went well, but the result of why I didn't have regular periods was a huge problem. I remember when Paul and my dad came into my hospital room; they looked very worried and sad. Then the doctor came in and explained to me what he discovered. He found streak ovaries. There wasn't enough of an ovary to produce my own eggs. My condition was called Primary Ovarian Failure (POF). He said I wouldn't be able to get pregnant right then, but most likely would be able to in the future when science and technology caught up to what I needed.

It really came down to the fact that I needed someone to donate their eggs to me. It's not the kind of thing you can go to the supermarket and purchase, like a dozen eggs for $2.99. My doctor asked if I had a sister who could donate her eggs to me. "No," I said, "I don't have a sister." Dr. Oliver said that in the future, maybe in another four to five years, there would most likely be some doctors with donor programs set up that could donate their extra eggs to help me *try* to get pregnant. The news was devastating. I wouldn't be able to get pregnant normally, and there was no hope for me for another four to five years. I cried so hard. It wasn't fair. Why was this happening to me? I wanted to give birth to our own children so desperately, and I knew I would be a great Mom and was looking forward to it so much. The news was heartbreaking, not only for myself and Paul but for my family as well. I asked the doctor why this had happened, but he told me there was no way of knowing for sure.

I felt so bad and so inadequate that I told Paul he should divorce me and find someone who could have a child with him. I was damaged goods. I cried and cried and cried. He tried to console me and reassure me that everything was going to be o.k., that he loved me very much and didn't want to divorce me. He said that "it didn't matter if we didn't have children of our own" and that "we could always adopt a child." It was so sweet of him to say that, but it was hard to explain to anyone else how I was feeling. I felt isolated and alone. It helped a little to hear that I had his emotional support, but I still felt insecure about the situation. He said we could adopt a child if we couldn't find anyone to donate their eggs to me, and he was trying very hard to be understanding, for which I was grateful. Paul was a wonderful husband, and I knew he would make a great father someday, and I just wanted to experience being pregnant and giving birth to our child. I wasn't emotionally ready to give up on the idea of trying for what would be biologically half his genes. After all, my doctor always said that even if our baby was only genetically half mine, he felt strongly that the child would have many characteristics and influences from me that would play a strong role in how our child would be. Maybe, later on, we could discuss adoption, but first I wanted to try and find a donor and try to get pregnant.

Questions and answers during my early teenage years were now falling into place. The under-development of my body was making more sense now. I liked boys, but they weren't as interested in me as much as I was in them. I had wanted a boyfriend so badly. There were a couple of boys in high school who I saw for a short time, but they didn't ever turn into something serious. My mom always said that my time would come, but for me, it wasn't soon enough. I hadn't developed as much as the other girls in school. Of course, the boys would be more interested in the other girls over me. I didn't understand what was wrong with me. Why was I different? All I knew is that my menstrual cycles were not normal, and I couldn't imagine ever letting anyone know about it. It was my secret that only my immediate family and best friend, Belinda, would know about for many years. When I graduated high school, I was four feet eleven inches and eighty-seven pounds. It felt normal to me, but looking back on things, I realize how tiny I really was compared to some of my friends. I was just a late bloomer. By the time I was twenty, I grew two inches and gained fifteen pounds and filled out somewhat. I felt more normal and womanly. Life was much better than the stressful and lonely teenage and young adult years, and I felt myself beginning to worry less about the fact that something going on in my body might be off.

In 1978, the first test tube baby was born. Her name was Louise Brown, and her birth in England opened the door for many thousands of children to be born to parents with infertility issues. I was still in high school then and wasn't even aware of the infertility issues I would be facing in the years to come. Five to six years later (around 1983 - 1984), after the first test tube baby was born, the technology still hadn't caught up with my fertility issues. Then, on February 3, 1984, there was a historical embryo transfer, and the world's first baby was born to an infertile woman from a donated embryo. This was around the time I had my laparoscopy to find out what my problem was. There was progress in this area, and although it was not fast enough for me, at least I could see there was hope for something in our future.

In the eighties, infertility was a taboo subject, and it was such an embarrassing subject for me. I never wanted to tell anyone why I couldn't get pregnant. I never wanted anyone to know my true problem; it was just too personal. I feared that someday, in a casual conversation, a co-worker would ask me a question like, "Why did you have to go to the doctor to get pregnant? What was your infertility problem?" For example, they might say "Oh, I have a cousin who is having trouble getting pregnant. Maybe she has the same infertility problem that you have, and maybe you can help her out with some information or know of a doctor who can help her also." It was just too scary to say it out loud what my problem was, so I never did. It's extremely personal.

Once I got used to the idea that I would have to have surgery to get pregnant, it allowed me to open up and admit at least that I had an infertility problem. Maybe I could help others with infertility issues and open up a dialog with them. Maybe my problem could help someone else find the help they needed in order for them to start a family also. I thought it might be a good idea to open up a little and started getting comfortable with that idea, until a very frightening phone call in 1995 that changed our lives forever. Here's how it all started

THE SEARCH IS ON

Would we ever be able to have a family of our own? What should we do? Do we wait for technology to catch up with my medical condition? Should we look into adoption? So many emotions, so much sadness, and insecurity. Compounding the situation were conversations about being a newlywed. Someone would always ask "So when are you going to start a family"? or "How many children do you want to have?" Paul and I both felt that emptiness inside of us that we might not ever have children of our own. We tried to just sluff off the conversation as not being a big deal, and not show others that we were feeling upset deep inside when they asked about it. We didn't want to tell anyone what our problem was and didn't want them to feel bad for us either. It wasn't their problem; it was ours. It was our very personal secret.

In August 1984 Paul and I bought our first home together. It was a brand-new home in Ontario, and we would visit the house on the weekends to see what progress the contractors had done on our house that week. It was fun to see it being built. It was a little farther away from our jobs than our apartment, but it was our dream home. During this time, we were both working at the Jet Propulsion Laboratory (JPL). Paul was still in computers, and I was in procurement. We drove into work together, and the drive was about forty-five to fifty minutes each day, one way. After about six months I decided to find work closer to our home. I started work for the regional office of Domino's Pizza Distribution Center in Ontario, California as an administrative assistant in the accounting department. It was less than five miles away, and I really liked it. Paul still made the drive into Pasadena. He was tougher than me and had a better paying job that he didn't want to give up.

Many of our neighbors were mostly young couples with small children or no children yet. It was the best neighborhood we ever lived in. I remember this one evening when we were at our neighbor's house celebrating them buying a jacuzzi. We were in our neighbors' backyard having fun in their jacuzzi and dancing around. Then Kim, one of our friends, announced that she was pregnant. Everyone was happy for her and started congratulating her, and Paul and I also sincerely conveyed our best wishes for her. What I didn't realize then, was that the host of that party noticed my face turn very sad when Kim announced her good news. I didn't realize that the sadness I was feeling was apparent to anyone else. He told me this a couple of years later when the neighbors were having a party for Paul and I after we told them that we were expecting a baby. It's funny how you respond to certain news, and you aren't even aware of any expression that might be showing. At the time, we were happy for her but sad for us at the same time. I guess I wasn't a very good actor and had a harder time than I thought hiding my feelings.

After hearing this news, we tried to put our sadness aside and were filled with a renewed sense of purpose, excitement and determination. We had been married for less than a year and had our whole life in front of us. Paul and I decided to calm down and wait to see what science and technology would turn up. From that point on, we were glued to the television whenever we heard there was any breaking news about infertility, and we would listen intently to the news reports whenever the infertility subject came up. The internet wasn't something that was around back then, so we relied heavily on waiting to see what the news would share. I remember putting a tape into the VCR to record the upcoming segment and sitting in front of the TV with a pad of paper ready to take notes just in case the VCR didn't work. I wanted to be informed and up-to-date with anything new about fertility treatments. Despite our eagerness to learn all we could, the information was often so vague that it didn't seem like there was any real progress happening at all.

We had been married for about two and a half years, and on March 29, 1986, my dad, while listening to KFWB on the radio, heard about a new International Infertility and Reproductive Clinic that was coming to Orange County, California. My dad and I usually spoke on the phone every week or two, and he told me about this segment he heard on the radio. I was excited to hear of the possibility of having this new facility so close to our home; that was only forty-five minutes from our house in Ontario.

I was so thankful that Dad heard this news. He knew how much we wanted to start a family, and it was really important to us. Deep down, I think he also really wanted to become a grandpa. He wrote down the information on a slip of paper and handed it to me the next time we saw each other, and I have kept that note for all these years. *Maybe this clinic would be an option for us,* I thought.

Not long after, my husband and I heard of a fertility program starting in Australia. We were willing to travel anywhere to have the chance to become pregnant, even though the program would probably be too expensive for us. Any news was good news. Time and again, I would hear about new fertility treatments, giving me the hope, I needed to keep searching for answers.

In October 1986, I was at my annual exam with my gynecologist, Dr. Oliver. He said he knew of a new start-up program for infertility and wanted to know if we would be interested in finding out more information. "Maybe they can help you," he told us. We learned that it was at the UCLA Medical Center in California, and he went on to say, "You know, Dr. Bill Yee had been doing some great work in infertility there." We were very interested, especially since UCLA was only about fifty miles from where we lived. Dr. Oliver wrote me a referral letter and sent my records to Dr. Bill Yee. We were so excited to meet with an official specialist that might be our answer! I can still remember walking down the halls of the office and sitting down with Dr. Yee, full of hope and excitement. I was expecting him to say that he had answers for us and we would begin coming to his clinic to start the process to get pregnant. Unfortunately, our dreams were dashed again, because his program wasn't set up for egg donors who weren't related to someone, yet.

It was hard to find out that Dr. Yee couldn't help me, but he did know of a doctor who was part of a small group of specialists developing new infertility techniques in Virginia. The doctor he knew of was from Texas, his name was Dr. Ricardo Asch. I had heard about a group of doctors working in Virginia, and my dad heard about a doctor relocating to Orange County. Was this the same group of doctors I heard of about five months ago? Could this be the doctor that would change our world? Dr. Asch was relocating to Southern California, and we were determined to meet him, completely unaware at the time of how much he would turn our lives upside down.

Life was like a roller coaster. The morning we met with Dr. Yee, I was "all in" for positive news from our appointment with him, and yet at the same morning our dreams were dashed, our spirits were simultaneously lifted when he said he would be writing a referral letter to Dr. Asch. That day was disappointing and hopeful at the same time. We just had to roll with the punches and keep a positive attitude, that someday, we would have the opportunity to try to conceive our own child. It didn't do any good to be distraught, I had to think positively that it would happen for us. Pregnancy was just a matter of time.

He was going to contact the new doctor coming to Orange County so Paul and I could meet with him. Dr. Yee wrote a very nice referral letter introducing me to Dr. Asch who had just moved from Texas to open a fertility clinic in Garden Grove, California who might have a donor egg program. We were so excited to finally have some hope. This was the best news we had heard in a very long time.

As soon as we receive the referral letter in the mail, I called Dr. Asch's office to make an appointment to meet with him. I was so excited to have another "lead" to a doctor who might be able to help us get pregnant. The appointment was set, and we scheduled the day off from work to meet this new doctor in town.

In October 1986, Paul and I met with Dr. Balmaceda, one of Dr. Asch's partners. I still remember to this day in vivid color, everything that happened when we met with him. There were boxes, filing cabinets, and office furniture scattered all around a temporary location that was set up downstairs while they waited for their offices upstairs to be completed. We were escorted to a conference room where Dr. Balmaceda, a very nice man from Chile, listened carefully to our infertility story and showed us compassion for everything we had been through. He took the time to look at my medical records we had brought with us. He said that *technology had finally caught up and there was a donor egg program starting at their facility.* I remember squealing with excitement! I was on cloud nine! He said that Paul would need testing also, but he was sure that Paul's sperm were going to be o.k. I asked Dr. Balmaceda "How would you know that?" He pointed to Paul's head that was obviously balding. Apparently balding was a good sign for good sperm. We all had a good laugh. It was one of the best days in our young married life so far.

That day, Dr. Balmaceda changed my estrogen and progesterone medication by increasing their amounts and wanted to begin monitoring my blood levels.   I'll never forget that day, the day we were finally on the road to having a baby. We took pictures standing outside of the office building for the nurses and doctors to match us up with a suitable donor. It was a moment to remember forever. After researching over twelve different infertility programs over the years, the hard work paid off, and we were getting the answers we had been longing for.

As hard as all of this was to go through, (especially with not having the current luxury of the internet to help) I am so glad we never gave up. It was worth the hours spent, the tears shed, and the hope we clung to that sometimes felt impossible to attain. Throughout our journey, each one of these doctors had something special to offer in the way of either hope, encouragement, information or a referral to another facility or doctor. Eventually, we too were pointed in the right direction. Can you imagine how many facilities there are today and how much easier it is to search for one now that we have the internet?

HOPE FOR A BABY

We left the office that day with our hopes and dreams lifted. Did this just happen? This new facility, The Center for Reproductive Health, gave us some pamphlets about their facility and instructions on their program. Our heads were spinning with shock and excitement. Then I was told to call the office every month to see if anyone else was cycling (ovulating) at the same time I was. Every month, before work, I drove to the doctor's office to have my blood drawn and have my hormone levels checked. I remember standing in their hallway before the office opened up at 7:00 am along with a line of other patients there who also had appointments. I wanted to be one of the first patients to sign in. The sooner I could have my blood drawn and leave, the sooner I could get to work and hopefully on time by 8:00 am. It was always a little frantic since the drive back to work was about forty-five minutes. This entire time, my employer didn't know that Paul and I were trying to conceive a baby by extreme measures. Many times, I was asked to have my blood drawn the week after my cycle had ended, and the following week also. That meant drawing blood sometimes three times in a month. My estrogen and progesterone levels needed monitoring very closely, just in case there was an egg donor cycling at the same time I was and would be able to accept the egg donation.

It was very early on in the egg donation process for donating to another recipient. The doctors weren't freezing embryos yet, so every donation had to be a direct donor to the recipient. Also, the donor needed to look somewhat like me. We wanted our child to blend as if it was our child that we made naturally. I guess I still felt the stigma of being infertile. Only our immediate family and my friend Belinda knew I couldn't get pregnant in the usual way. I always had that fear of someone asking me what my infertility problem was, and I never wanted to tell anyone what had really gone on. It seemed like it was too private for anyone outside my close circle to know about, and I didn't want to have that conversation with anyone.

I felt like I was a guinea pig, having so many blood tests and following their protocol. I'm sure that all the blood draws provided data for the doctors to see what brought a successful pregnancy and what hormone levels a woman's body needed to have to maintain the pregnancy. Everything at that time was a "first" in the world of infertility. I was willing to go through it all to try to carry our child.

These visits went on for almost nine months, as Paul and I waited for some good news of a possible donor. We thought it would never happen. Waiting for so long, every month, month after month, hoping for some good news, any possibility that it would someday be our turn to try to get pregnant, started to feel farther and farther away. Then one day, in July 1987 I was at the doctor's office for monthly routine blood tests, and I mentioned to the staff and nurses how long we had been waiting. I was getting so frustrated that it would never happen for us. One of the nurses said "You should talk to Dr. Asch again to see if he can do anything." I didn't think that talking to him would change anything. I was already his patient; he should have known that I had been coming to his office for blood tests for nine months already. Why would one more conversation make any difference? Regardless, Paul and I made an appointment so that we could speak with him in person.

We had spoken with him many times in the office as he was there for a short time before going to do surgery at the hospital. Dr. Asch was a tall, very slim, nice looking man with black hair who was always very kind and personable with us and would sit down and look me straight in the eyes ask me how I was feeling and make small talk. He truly did care about helping us. He appeared to balance his time with his office patients as well as needing to get to the hospital for a surgery. His office and lab staff seemed a little more rushed as they went about their daily work., and the office was a little chaotic at times with so many patients coming and going. Even though Dr. Asch wasn't a celebrity, he had a certain celebrity presence, to us at least. We felt he held our future in his hands. I know that I was always happy when I got to see him, even if it was just seeing him dashing out of one door and into the next.

It was July 1987 and Paul went with me to the next appointment, and we had a chance to meet with Dr. Asch for a short visit. We sat with him and had a very strange conversation. We told Dr. Asch how long we had been waiting, that we were getting discouraged, but wanted to have a baby and start a family together. He said he understood that it was a difficult process to go through. He asked us, "If you are able to have a baby, would you *love* the child?" "Yes, of course," we replied. We explained that, for us, it would be the best thing in the world to be parents and to start a family of our own. We wanted it so much. I'm not sure why he asked us this. It was kind of strange and seemed out of place. Maybe he wanted to test us to see if we really wanted a child and would be good parents. Maybe it was his way of justifying what his purpose was in creating new life for those who would never experience it otherwise. I'm not sure exactly what he was thinking, but it was a funny and odd question to be asking us. How could you not love your child? Then he said, "I might have something for you on your next cycle." That day, he increased my estrogen and progesterone levels for a possible GIFT (Gamete Intrafallopian Transfer) procedure the following month. My hormone levels needed to be higher so my body would be ready to accept the egg transfer. I was elated!! Finally, it might be our turn to get pregnant.

The following month, in early August, I was at the doctor's office again for my routine blood tests. This time the nurse said that Dr. Asch told her there might be eggs for me in about two weeks. I was told to be ready on August 24, 1987, for a phone call about a possible transfer of eggs. It was hard to believe what I was hearing. Could this really be happening for us? Was it finally our time? I so thrilled by this news, I felt like I was floating on the clouds and couldn't come down to earth. My day at work was a total blur. I couldn't wait to tell Paul about my doctor's appointment. That evening I filled him in on everything that went on at the appointment. He wanted a play by play description of the visit. I described which nurses and doctors were at the office that day, what they were doing and how the conversation went when the nurse told me about being ready in two weeks for a possible egg transfer. Paul said he wished he was with me that day to hear everything in person. Paul's parents would be celebrating their 50th wedding anniversary in a couple of weeks, and we already planned to fly to Florida to surprise his parents at a family dinner. We planned to walk into the restaurant with a video camera running while the entire family was already seated for dinner and surprise his parents. We only had that Friday, Saturday, Sunday, and Monday, because possibly that next week we would be having surgery and getting pregnant! When it rains, it pours, even with good things! It was overwhelming to have so much suddenly going on at once, but we knew we could handle it, even as we were beside ourselves with joy.

We flew to Florida and had a very nice but short visit with the family, and then back to work the next week, only to work a few days knowing that I might be off work the following week if there were eggs for me and if I had surgery. It was a very intense time, and it was hard to keep all of this quiet from my co-workers, but I did. It was that stigma of infertility hanging over my head, and I didn't want to have to say what my infertility problem was. I wasn't ready for that. I just figured that if they heard that I had to have surgery to get pregnant, the next question would be: Why? What's wrong with you? So many things could have gone wrong; I was worried that with everything, I still might not even get pregnant. Many couples aren't successful in getting pregnant when they start the fertility treatments, and we wanted to play it safe.

The morning of August 24th, Paul and I both started our days out normally, going to our jobs. Then, I got the long-awaited phone call at work that morning. The nurse was on the line when I answered. She said "Get here to the office as quickly as possible. There are donated eggs waiting for you!

It was my turn for the GIFT procedure to try to become pregnant. I called Paul and listening to the phone ring, my heart hammering in my chest. I heard his voice on the other end of the line, and before he could say two words I exclaimed, "Hurry up and come home now! We have to go to the hospital. It's time to get pregnant!" He rushed home, and so did I. Then we drove as fast as possible to the doctor's office. We couldn't believe it was finally happening for us. We were going to have a baby!

First things first, Paul had to make his contribution to the procedure. He was embarrassed but went semi-cheerfully to a room where a nurse stood outside waiting for him to hand her his sperm in a little cup. He sheepishly gave it to her, and she rushed it off to the lab.

While I was waiting in another room, the nurse was telling me about the donor. She was excited for us about this particular donor. She said the match couldn't have been more perfect. We looked like we could be sisters. She was twenty-four years old with hair the same color as mine, about 5' 4" and very pretty. I thought she sounded perfect, but it was hard to think straight as my mind was spinning with excitement. I wondered what the surgery was going to be like. How was it going to feel when I was pregnant? I was absolutely positive that I was going to get pregnant. I believed in going into this procedure thinking very positively. No doubts at all, it was going to work. Paul came into the room, and I told him what the nurse said about the donor. He was happy about everything too.

The nurse came back in and said we needed to go next door to the Garden Grove Hospital and Medical Center for the procedure, that the doctors were waiting for me there. I couldn't believe how quickly things were suddenly going! The procedure they were doing was cutting edge technology, created by the elite group of doctors back east. There had been much success with this technique, and it was my best chance for me to achieve pregnancy.

The doctors fill your belly with gas so they can see everything inside using a laparoscope. The eggs and sperm are put into a catheter and inserted into the Fallopian tubes. Then they travel naturally through the Fallopian tubes and implant in the Uterine wall. Voilà! A baby begins growing! There were about ten doctors and nurses in the operating room helping to facilitate this procedure. It was such an ordeal! Even after all these years, I can still feel being wheeled down the hall into the operating room. I remember what it looked like inside and when they put the IV in me and told me to count backward from a hundred. I don't think I got past ninety-seven, and I was out. When surgery was over, I remember a nurse speaking loudly, helping me wake back up. She said that my surgery was over, and I would be going back to my room shortly. I was still so very excited and felt so lucky to be given the opportunity to have this procedure. It was a huge ordeal, for someone to actually donate a part of themselves to me, so Paul and I could possibly have a family of our own. That woman was so special and incredible to us.

Afterward, Dr. Asch visited us in my hospital room. "Everything during the procedure went well, and things look promising," he said. "I truly think you will become pregnant." Of course, it was too early to know, but it sounded good to us. They were wonderfully positive words for me to think about every minute of the day for the next two weeks until they drew my blood again. This time for a pregnancy test.

I took it easy the rest of the week and stayed home from work, relaxed around the house watching TV while thinking and saying positive words like *I am pregnant.* I believed in positive thinking. I prayed that I was truly pregnant and it sure didn't hurt anything by thinking positively. Paul took such good care of me by making me dinner after work each night. He wouldn't let me lift or do anything. He even carried my purse for me!

It was a very long two weeks after the surgery, waiting to find out if I was pregnant, but finally, it was time for the big blood test to see if I would get a positive result. I drove to Garden Grove Medical Center early before work that day, as I had many times before, to have my blood drawn. As I left, they said they would call me when the results came in. I was so anxious waiting for that phone call, it was difficult to think straight, my entire body was nervous with excitement. I hadn't told my manager that I had this procedure to get pregnant; all I said was that I had a laparoscopic procedure done the week I was out of the office. They never asked any questions. That afternoon, I received a call from the doctor's office with the answer I had been waiting so very long for: I was pregnant! I remember squealing with excitement, not even sure what to do with myself. He said my Human Chorionic Gonadotropin (hCG) levels were very high and there was a good chance that I was having more than one baby. I couldn't believe it; I was completely overjoyed. I had been thinking positively the entire two weeks hoping for this result. I did receive three eggs the day of the procedure, so anything could happen. Now Paul and I would have to wait another two weeks to see how many babies it was going to be. *How many?* I thought to myself. One, two, three or more? We knew something like this could happen, and we did purchase a four-bedroom house in case we were lucky enough to have a family of our own. I called Paul at work and told him the good news. He was so excited! We were so lucky for this procedure to work on the first try. Some couples have to go through the procedure many times before getting pregnant. It felt like it was meant to be.

I told my manager and co-workers the good news, and they were thrilled for us too. After work, Paul and I celebrated at a Mexican restaurant. At dinner, we talked about every moment leading up to our chance to become pregnant. We recounted the time when I found out that I didn't have any ovaries to produce any eggs and how devastating that felt, and how it had been such a long road to get to where we were that day. We had been married almost four years at that point, and that's how long my first doctor said it would be before technology caught up with what I needed to get pregnant. We remembered all of the doctors we reached out to for information or scheduled appointments with. It was a lot of work that took a toll on our minds and emotions. It was hard, but we never gave up, and we now had a real chance to hold our precious baby or babies in our arms. Paul and I sure waited a long time for it to happen, but the waiting paid off, and we had truly been blessed. We told our neighbors when we got home that night, and they were also very excited for us. Then they surprised us by making a banner that said "Congratulations Paul and Joyce, Baby on the Way!" and hung it across the garage, and they also planned a party for us. It was great and is still one of my favorite memories.

In the beginning, there were many ultrasound appointments as well as the blood tests to make sure the pregnancy was progressing. A month after the GIFT procedure, the doctors would be able to see "how many" embryos were growing. That's when they said we were having twins.

It was amazing watching them grow. Sometimes it was hard to believe that we were having two babies, twins, and they would be here sooner than we were probably ready for. We felt very blessed that everything was turning out so well, that we were going to have the family that we had wanted so badly. At one of the ultrasound appointments, the doctors were using a new ultrasound machine with a vaginal probe. They said it was cutting edge technology and would show better ultrasound pictures too. Just then, the doctors said, "Wow, look at that!" "What?" I replied. The ultrasound technician was able to see both sides of the babies' brains. They had never seen the right and left hemispheres so clearly before in an ultrasound. They were so excited that they called four other doctors into this small exam room to see for themselves. It was weird having so many doctors in one room standing around me in such an embarrassing position. Oh well, chalk it up to technology advancing very quickly. From that point on, there were many times I felt like a guinea pig, but it was worth it.

DURING THE PREGNANCY

For the most part, the pregnancy was fairly normal. Normal if you count morning sickness and cravings for Mexican food and chocolate. What was unusual was that Paul had to give me a Progesterone injection in my hip every day for one hundred days so I could maintain the pregnancy. My body didn't produce progesterone naturally, so I had to take it in an oil formula with a big needle. The needle really was big. It had to be, to dispense the progesterone that was in a thick sesame oil or peanut oil. Unfortunately, I was allergic to it. I broke out in hives, and I itched so bad that I had welts. I itched from my toes to my tongue. It was awful, but I had to put up with it because if I didn't keep taking the progesterone, I would lose the babies. I wasn't going to risk losing them. Back in the eighties, the doctors weren't sure how long I needed to take the shots. I really was their guinea pig. They said to take them for a hundred days; that should be long enough. The doctors weren't sure at that time when the placenta took over and maintained the pregnancy on its own, so I followed orders and had progesterone shots for one-hundred days, along with the allergic reactions. I've heard from others going through similar infertility procedures more currently that they have the shots for around thirty days now. It's amazing to see what a big difference there is now in the length of time things take for certain treatments! The most encouraging thing about hearing these stories for me is that now I can look back, and recognize my contribution to science, to paving the way for hundreds of thousands of babies who have been born afterward; whose parents needed a little bit of extra help conceiving. I'm very proud of being able to contribute to this. Knowing the heartache an infertile couple goes through, deciding whether to proceed with fertility procedures or deciding to take another route is an incredibly rough journey. Making those decisions is never easy.

I remember the first ultrasound that Paul was able to attend. It was November 17, 1987. It was such an event! I wrote notes on paper after the appointment so I could always remember it, and I figured I'd put them into the baby scrapbook. The babies were about two and a half months' gestation. We had one baby who was very active that day. We called that one Wiggles. Wiggles turned sideways and showed the spine and all the vertebrae, and then flipped around again, and we saw the legs, head, and cute little butt. Wiggles was a real show off. I'm not sure which twin it was, but I'm guessing that it was Heather wiggling around because the other twin was very sleepy, and Kevin ended up being a very sound sleeper his entire life. "Sleepy" didn't want to move or turn at all that day. I asked the doctor to wake him up. Dr. Balmaceda poked him a little bit, and that got him to move his arm and turn his body. The doctor said they were both healthy and had strong heartbeats, that everything was fine. In fact, he said they were "hefty" babies for almost three months, which was very good. They were about four inches long by that point and were adorable. We loved them already and couldn't wait until they arrived so that we could hold them in our arms.

Sometime around fifteen to seventeen weeks' gestation, doctors will order an Alpha–Fetoprotein (AFP) test. The AFP test is a normal test they do at this stage in pregnancy to see if the chromosomes are normal and to check for a possibility of Down Syndrome or Spina Bifida where certain major deformities could be detected at that age. To me, it was just another blood test. I had so many of them; it had become routine for me. I had actually forgotten about this particular test. Then right before the long Christmas holiday weekend, we received a letter in the mail that my AFP levels were abnormally high, and we were to call the doctor and make an appointment to discuss the test results. We tried contacting the doctor's office, but their answering service just took a message and told us there wasn't any way to contact the doctor to see what the test results meant due to a long holiday weekend. I guess our message wasn't important enough to pass along to the doctor because we never heard back from him. It wasn't until the next regular business workday that we got a hold of anyone. All we knew is that there could be a problem with the babies. We were so afraid. Those several days were filled with so much worry, and I knew it wasn't healthy to worry. It was so nerve-wracking and scary to not be able to reach the doctor all weekend; it was just awful.

After a very long couple of days, I called the doctor's office and finally spoke with him. He didn't seem to be concerned at all. My doctor said that apparently, the AFP levels could be higher because of having more than one baby, but we needed to check into it further. He arranged for me to have an amniocentesis. They do this by sticking a needle into the amniotic sac through the belly and withdrawing a small amount of amniotic fluid to test for abnormalities in the chromosomes. Simple, right? I wasn't so sure. I hadn't been concerned with other procedures in the past, but somehow this test was different. It seemed much riskier.

I scheduled an appointment at the UCLA Medical Center for this test. First, the doctor did an ultrasound to look at the baby's spine looking for any abnormalities. He said the babies looked good and the doctor asked if we wanted to know the sexes of the babies. We did. He said we were having a girl and a boy. Wow!! It couldn't have been more perfect. After we got that news, we had to decide if we were going to let them stick a needle in me. The doctor did explain that there was a risk of bringing on premature labor with this test, which was information we weren't prepared to hear. Paul and I said we wanted some time to think about it. I got dressed, and I remember very clearly walking the halls at the hospital with my husband, discussing what were we going to do. We had a huge decision to make, and the doctors were pushing us to do the test. "Do we want to risk losing them by having this procedure done?" we asked each other. It was one of the most important decisions of our lives, and we had such a short time to decide. They were waiting for us to return to their office and tell them our decision. We asked ourselves if the test results showed there was a problem, would we decide to end the pregnancy? That answer was a definite NO. We would deal with whatever the babies needed. We loved our children so much even before they were born and would take care of them no matter the outcome of the test.

We told the doctor we decided not to have the test. He appeared upset with us. After discussing it with him more, the doctor confessed that he needed the test done because it helped the hospital with their statistics for abnormal AFP tests, and his employer was pushing for the tests to be performed. We asked him point blank, "Are you telling us that this test is more for your reports rather than the benefit of our family?" Here was a doctor working at a major medical center (UCLA Medical Center) and his superior has put him in a position to perform an amniocentesis on all patients as to collect data. He looked almost ashamed at that moment as he sat facing us. He said that we would benefit from the procedure if there *were* something wrong, that there might be some early intervention the doctors could do so the babies wouldn't be born with any problems. Then we asked him "What did you think of the ultrasound? Did you see anything abnormal?" The doctor looked at us and replied, "The babies look good." We appreciated his honesty, and with this information, we decided to leave the hospital without having an amniocentesis. It was a very traumatic experience having to decide something so important, especially with so little time, and the risk was all on us, not the doctor or the hospital. We weren't going to risk losing the pregnancy. Paul and I were proud of ourselves that we made the best decision for our family. It was a very difficult and emotionally draining day.

A few more weeks went by, and I was experiencing a heaviness in my pelvic area, and my doctor explained that my cervix was softening and shortening. He told me that I was going into premature labor and might need to go onto bed rest. It was terrifying to hear that, but he suggested a treatment to try and slow things down.

"Let's try Brethine pills," he said, "and see how your body reacts. Maybe it will be enough to control the mini contractions you have been feeling. The medicine might make you feel jittery at first, but you should get used it." We agreed, and I started the medication. He was right, I did feel a little jittery for the first couple of days but was fine afterward. It was a good thing that we decided not to go through with the amniocentesis that day. It had only been a few weeks since that appointment, and I was now on the edge of premature labor. I felt we surely made the right decision that day. It could have easily ended in catastrophe.

At my next doctor's visit, a week later I told him how I reacted to the pills, and he thought I should try something different. I said that I was used to them, and felt fine and wanted to continue taking them, but he insisted that I try Magnesium Gluconate. He said that Magnesium Gluconate had been showing great results in slowing down premature labor and he had been doing a lot of research on the drug and was very pleased with the results. He made a big deal about it and called in a prescription to the hospital pharmacy so that I could start on them right away. We rushed over to get the prescription filled, and the pharmacist came out to talk to us. He said he could fill the prescription, but this Magnesium Gluconate was an over the counter vitamin supplement, and I didn't need a prescription for it. He asked us if we still wanted him to fill it. We told him how the doctor made such a big deal out of it, that we thought we'd better have it filled to follow doctor's orders. I began taking the new prescription I had been given, and within twelve hours I was in real labor that could not be stopped. Taking it was the beginning of the end of the pregnancy. From that point forward, our new life motto was, "In God We Trust, In Doctors We Ask Questions."

THE BEGINNING OF THE END

A routine day turned out to be the worst day of our lives. I remember having dinner that night at a restaurant called Spires in Ontario, California. We had been there many times before for breakfast and dinner. We ate a lot of breakfasts and dinners at Spires, and I also lost a lot of meals after eating there (because of the pregnancy, not because the food was bad.) In fact, my favorite meal there was the Eggs Benedict with the eggs scrambled. It didn't stay with me very long, but it was worth it!

At dinner, we were discussing the fact that I had been feeling a lot of light contractions and maybe we should go to the hospital, although we felt dumb going because we had just seen the doctor that afternoon, and we shouldn't have anything to be worried about. After all, I was now on a new prescription to slow the contractions, and it should be working. The doctor surely knew what he is doing, right? He made such a big deal out of this prescription and had even taken me off of Brethine that _was_ working for me. I began to question if maybe he shouldn't have done that.

I had a second job as a Mary Kay Consultant and had an order to deliver that night. It wasn't far from the restaurant, so we decided to deliver her order and then if I was still feeling contractions, we would go to the hospital to make sure everything was alright. An hour passed, and as I was still feeling them, we went back to the hospital so that I could get checked out.

They admitted me to Loma Linda University Medical Center right away. I had dilated two to three centimeters, and they said I wasn't going home. They tried to slow down the labor because it was too early to deliver. I was only twenty-five weeks' gestation, and there wasn't much chance of survival for the babies if I delivered that early. Also, having twins meant that a twenty-five-week-old twin could be smaller than a single birth at that same gestation. I was determined to stay pregnant and go all the way to forty weeks. I still believed in positive thinking. Paul and I explained to the hospital what we had gone through to get pregnant, and how long we had waited for our chance. We begged them to do anything they could to help stop the contractions. It's hard to understand that earlier in the day, everything was going well, and then taking the advice of my obstetrician to start this Magnesium Gluconate, that he was so proud of from his own research studies, would begin the end of my pregnancy. It's maddening when we look back on it. We still wish that we hadn't followed our doctor's orders that day.

I remember thinking that everything was going to be o.k., that I'd be able to hold onto the pregnancy for the entire term. It never occurred to me how much danger I was in and how close to the end of my pregnancy I was. I was given Magnesium Sulfate (MagSulfate) to control the contractions, and it did work for a couple of days. In fact, the doctor's prescribed so much MagSulfate that I couldn't move. I felt paralyzed and so numb that I felt like "Gumby." I was like a ragdoll, limp and could only speak with slurred words. Then I felt like I had to go the bathroom very badly, but the nurses weren't sure it was a need to urinate, or if I was having a contraction, so the doctor on call catheterized me, and I felt much better afterward. So, I guess I did have to go after all. My muscles were so relaxed that I just couldn't do it on my own.

The nurses were getting very worried about my physical condition, and they notified the doctor and updated him on how I was doing. He wanted to change me over to a calcium channel blocker, but the hospital was afraid that was too drastic. They thought it could kill me. Calcium channel blockers have been used to relax blood vessels and increase the supply of blood and oxygen to the heart while also reducing the heart's workload. I don't know why this was so problematic to them, but they were definitely worried. They didn't agree with him and went above his head to the Chief of Obstetrics to make a change in my care. They were really mad about the decisions my doctor was making. They said that if the calcium channel block wasn't done correctly, I could go into cardiac arrest. They were against putting me on the calcium channel blocker at all but were eventually convinced to reduce the Mag Sulfate and introduce the calcium blocker slowly, kind of like stepping on the clutch of a car and easing onto the gas. It had to be done gradually to prevent any ill effects. I was on so much Mag Sulfate that I wonder if it has affected my thinking ability and memory to this day. I felt so disconnected from my mind and body during that time. I'm glad the nurses and other doctors came to my rescue. As soon as I was weaned off of the Mag Sulfate, I started feeling like my old self again. I felt so much better.

Within a day of that, I had to deliver our daughter Heather because I had dilated to around seven to eight centimeters, and they weren't able to stop the contractions any longer. It was a very scary time and the last night I was pregnant with her; we had even scheduled our first Lamaze class for that evening. I didn't know what I was supposed to do. How do I push out this baby? I felt really silly while pushing when I had a contraction. I'd push my stomach out, and nothing happened. Then I remember hearing a nurse say, "push like you have a bowel movement." Oh, that's how you do it? Duh! I think everything happened very quickly after that, and Heather was born. I was lying flat in the operating room and couldn't see all the hustle and bustle around me, but Paul said the doctors whisked her away quickly, and that he saw her for only a microsecond right before they handed her to the Neonatal Intensive Care Unit (NICU) team who was waiting for her. Then we asked ourselves, "Did she cry?" We weren't sure but didn't think so.

Heather was born on February 2, 1988, at 10:07 in the morning at twenty-five and a half weeks gestation. She was delivered naturally with an episiotomy and was whisked away so quickly that I didn't even get to see her. Later on, the nurses brought me pictures of her. She was so tiny and so pretty...one pound twelve ounces and eleven inches long. I loved her so much and prayed so hard that she would be alright. She was my little miracle, and it was only the beginning. Although Heather had been born already, I was still pregnant with our son. I stayed in the operating room for a couple of hours after delivering Heather, as the doctors needed to see if I was going to have to deliver him. They were hoping to hold off the contractions so I could stay pregnant with him for as long as possible. They were successful, and they returned me to my room for rest.

It was exciting to finally have our baby girl but frightening because she was born so early and was so tiny. In 1988, babies born before twenty-eight weeks usually didn't survive. I stayed calm and positive that everything would be alright. The next morning, they brought me more pictures of her and said she was doing well and was sleeping on her waterbed comfortably. They asked me if I wanted to see her. I responded, "Well yes, of course!" I was so excited to see her; it was the highlight of my day.

The nurses wheeled me down the long hallway on a gurney to see Heather. Paul had the video camera rolling to capture everything. It was exciting! We were going to see our daughter! It would be my first time to see her. I couldn't sit up because I was still pregnant and trying to hold on to our son for as long as possible. We were introduced to Heather's nurse, and she explained what everything in her incubator was for, and how it was helping Heather get stronger.

I was trying to hang on to every word the nurse was saying, but it was a very special time, and I was feeling distracted for everything I was being told because I just had to stare at Heather. She was so beautiful. I remember so clearly holding her tiny little hand, and how she squeezed my finger. She also seemed to respond to my voice. Heather knew that I was her mommy and that I was with her. There is truly a connection between an unborn child and its mother and knowing who that person is on the outside. It was amazing. Paul and I talked to her, and she wiggled around a little bit as if she was trying to communicate with us. She was so little and very dark red. Her hair was a very dark brown, and she had a cute little pink hat on her head to keep her warm. It was hard to see her hooked up to the IV's and tubes and monitors. Everything was so big compared to her tiny size. My love for her was unimaginable. At that moment I didn't have any contractions or pain that I was aware of. I could have stayed there all day just watching her, but I knew I needed to rest and let the nurses take care of her while I took care of our son Kevin. I didn't want to leave her, but I knew that I had to rest.

As I was about to leave, I noticed her nurse getting teary-eyed and that she seemed a little upset. I didn't know why, and I didn't ask. I assumed that those types of visits were emotional for the nursing staff, and not just the parents. What they didn't tell us, was in between the time she was doing well in the morning and when they asked me if I wanted to see her, they gave Heather fluids because her potassium levels were too high. Well, they gave her too much, and they caused a bleed on her brain. At that point, her life had changed forever. Her quality of life would have been diminished forever with many disabilities. We didn't know that they gave her too many fluids at the time. In fact, we didn't find out for many weeks later that this had happened. One of Kevin's nurses told us when we were visiting him in the hospital this had happened and knew since she had been one of Heather's nurses also. It seemed like one bad thing after another was happening.

INFANT LOSS AWARENESS

A few hours passed since we visited her, and the doctors came into my room to say that her Patent Ductus Arteriosus (PDA) had opened up and they needed to do surgery to close it. This PDA is a hole in the aorta that normally closes when a baby takes its first breath. The doctors told us that Heather's PDA did close. However, it opened up later on. They sometimes treat this with medicine or surgery to close the hole. She needed surgery. There are some hospitals where they fix the PDA right at the incubator site as to not stress the baby any more than possible. At Loma Linda University Medical Center, their guideline was to take the baby to an operating room. Well at that time, part of the hospital was under construction. In fact, I could hear jack hammering the entire time I had been admitted to the hospital four days earlier.

They came to us to tell us they were preparing Heather for surgery and were just waiting for an operating room to open up for her. While waiting, however, she became unstable, and they said they couldn't do the surgery, that there wasn't anything more they could do for her. They told me she was going to die. They said they were very sorry and asked if we wanted to hold her. It was hard to believe what we were hearing at that moment. How could everything turn for the worse so quickly? We had just seen her a few hours earlier, and it was so fantastic and exciting and surreal. It was the best experience I had had in the past few days. A team of doctors and nurses brought Heather to Paul and me in my hospital room. It was really strange having so many people standing around us, but that was how the hospital did things when someone was going to die. Their philosophy was to have a supportive team around the patient in an extremely difficult situation. I just thought the room was too crowded during a very personal and private time of saying goodbye to our daughter forever. The nurse was "bagging" her (giving her oxygen), and the doctor kept checking her breaths and heartbeat as we were holding her in our arms and talking to her telling her how much we loved her and that everything was going to be alright. We told her that we were going to miss her so much and were so sorry she had to suffer through this. It was so strange that we were even having this conversation. It didn't seem real. Why was this was happening to us all? It just shouldn't be happening! Once her breaths slowed and her heart was quiet, they stopped bagging her. She was gone forever. We cried and held her as we held each other for the last time. I still couldn't believe that she died. Everything seemed fine hours earlier, filled with hope and dreams for the future for our daughter.

It didn't seem real that she was now gone. We held her in our arms for a while until the nurses said they needed to take her. I know I would have held her in my arms all night if I could. I never wanted to let her go. Life wasn't fair. We lost our first-born child. Our beautiful daughter, Heather, lived for a short day and a half. All the words on earth will never be able to describe how horrible that was.

Moments ago, the room had been filled with several doctors, nurses, the chaplain, my husband and our little girl, and now it was empty. It was just Paul and me taking in the day's events of what had happened. Did it happen? Couldn't we go back and change what had just happened? Then we remembered that I was still pregnant with our son. Since I was the best incubator for him, I had to stay calm and not freak out and lose control of my emotions. That seemed so unnatural to be calm when we had just lost our daughter. I wanted to cry and fall apart, but I knew I couldn't. I had to hold it together for our son. I had to hold onto him for as long as possible.

The nurses kept checking on me and asking me how I felt "down there." They were concerned that I could go into labor because of all the stress I had just experienced. I remember praying a lot and asking for God to keep our little boy safe and keep me pregnant for a very long time. It was one of the worst days of my life, but I had to keep going. Giving up was not an option.

PEACE AND REASONING AT LAST

My emotions and feelings and pain of the day we lost Heather continued for many years. Actually, for about ten years, until one day I was watching a television program where I heard someone talk about one way to get over the loss of someone. My ears perked up, and I was curious to hear the answer. He said to "remember all of the good times you had together." Those words spoke to me that day. It sounded so simplistic, but it felt like a lightbulb had just turned on in my brain. I think one has to arrive at a certain place in their healing and grieving process to be able to hear suggestions and be open to thinking about applying them. It was my time, and I was willing to try it. I started thinking about the time I did have with her. It was only a day and a half, but it was much longer when I was pregnant with her, and all the planning to be able to have her in the first place. No matter how short or long I was blessed to experience my daughter, I was going to be happy for the moments I had with her and just dwell on those good feelings. From that point forward, I thought about the times I felt her growing inside of me and how happy I was to experience being pregnant with her and her brother. I thought about the first time I felt those little flutters in my stomach and it made me smile. I was pregnant, and we were going to welcome beautiful children into this world. We got to visit her and talk to her and touch her when she was still with us, and that was such a special moment. At that time, we had no idea that things were going to turn badly within a few hours. Thinking about all of this made me cry a lot, but the tears were different. They were different because I cried and then I was able to smile. I was able to smile because I was now dwelling on the happy moments and felt so very thankful that we had that time together. That day was a real turning point for me in healing that hole I had in my heart for so long.

KEVIN

It was hard to sit in that grief, as well as experience the anticipation of our second child. Paul and I were both feeling so many things at once. I was still pregnant, extremely sad, and had to be strong and not fall apart because I had another life inside of me who was depending on me, and we wanted him so badly to be alright and to survive. Paul was grieving, and he was still having to drive to work every day, and it was a long way to Pasadena and then all the way to Loma Linda (almost 200 miles a day) after work to visit me. Looking back on things it was incredible that he could keep up that schedule for all three of us. On one of those tiring days, my brother Larry came to visit and keep Paul company. Larry stayed the night at our house. They always had a good time with each other and always got along so well. It's like they had been brothers before Paul and I ever got married. It was so nice that Larry wanted to be there for us, he was such a big help just by being around. Very early the next morning, the nurses thought that I had had a difficult night with contractions and thought that Paul needed to come back to the hospital right away. Well, Larry was a deep sleeper and didn't get up very easily. Somehow, Paul got Larry to wake up and get into the car quickly. I don't know how he did it, but whatever he said worked, and they headed for the hospital. Paul drove very fast that morning back to the hospital. He drove so fast that he thought he was going to get a ticket, but he didn't. They made it to the hospital in time to find out that I was still holding on to the pregnancy. What seemed like a close call was not. Pregnancy is a funny thing where there can be a lot of false alarms before the big event.

Several more days passed, and the head of the hospital came to visit us. He said there was only one other documented case at their hospital, and one other case in the world, where a woman had held onto the pregnancy for three days after delivering the first twin. I told him that I was going to hold on for a full-term pregnancy at forty weeks. I had only fourteen and a half weeks to go. He said he liked my positive attitude and wished me the best.

Since I had delivered naturally, the doctors left Heather's placenta in me. They didn't know if it was separate from our son's placenta, or if they were attached, if they tried to deliver her placenta, it might tear his, and that would be the end for him too. Thankfully I was the perfect pregnant patient. I did everything I was told to do. I was determined to stay pregnant for as long as possible. In fact, I was so perfect that I'm sure I was incredibly annoying. If the doctor or nurse on call said my Terbutaline shots were to be every four hours, and they weren't on time, I was pushing the buzzer for someone to give it to me.

Then Paul had a great idea; he bought a timer so I could monitor the nurses and remind them when it was time to give me another shot. The nurses were always getting busy, and I was always getting my shot late. It's not that I wanted the shot, but I needed the shot to hold off the contractions. I knew it would take them a little while to come to my room, so I would buzz them every ten minutes after the four hours were up when it was time for my shot. The timer did help because the nurses knew that I would be bugging them if they weren't there soon. It worked! I think that, subconsciously, they didn't want to have to give me another shot because my arms were already so bruised - so much so that the nurses would comment that my arms looked like a human pin cushion. I ended up being able to hold off delivering our son for **eleven days and seven hours**. We did break the hospital record (and world record) at that time, for delivering twins that many days apart – eleven days and seven hours in 1988!

The morning of February 13, 1988, I was feeling much better from the night before, when I had been having a lot of contractions. The contractions were controlled by 7:00 am, and I felt great. The nurse drew blood to check my white blood cell count since it had been running higher than normal.

Then an ultrasound was done to check on Kevin. I told the doctors I didn't feel him move very much the day before and all during the night. They discovered I had lost almost all the amniotic fluid and Kevin was under stress. At the time of the ultrasound, I didn't know what was happening. I only knew that something was very different. Shortly afterward I received a phone call from Dr. Valenzuela saying the baby was under stress. If I didn't deliver him right away, he might die inside me. He also said the doctors could take care of a sick baby outside of me, but not a dead one inside of me. That made a huge impression on me. It was clear that it was time to deliver him, and that my pregnancy with him was now over.

Kevin was born eleven days and seven hours after Heather was born. I made it to twenty-seven weeks gestation which is a long way from forty weeks, but that was the best my body would do. We were so hoping I could make it until at least twenty-eight weeks where the survival rate was much better, but that wasn't happening. Something else the doctors told us was that premature boys don't do as well as the premature girls. Hearing that was such a scary thought. We thought we were going to lose him as well, so when we had to deliver him, it felt like another death sentence all over again, but it was time. We couldn't delay it any longer, and we were so scared.

We made phone calls to family to let them know what was happening. Mom and Jack (my stepdad), Larry and Kelly (my brother and his girlfriend), and Dad and Barbara (my stepmom) all came to the hospital for the big event. They gave me Pitocin and an epidural, and I quickly dilated to eight or nine centimeters, and it was time to deliver. How ironic that for many weeks I had been taking medicine to hold off the contractions, and now everything needed to be sped up to get him out of me. It only took eleven minutes to push Kevin out. They had to use forceps because he was showing signs of stress by his heart rate dropping. We had gone through so much and had come so far...we couldn't lose him now. When he came out, he cried, and I saw him for the first time. He was weak but alive. They rushed him to the Neonatal Intensive Care Unit (NICU) to a pass-through window where the doctors were waiting for him. Paul and I looked at each other when we heard him cry. It was the best cry in the entire world. To us, that cry meant he was strong and had a fighting chance because his lungs had developed enough to make that sound. Both placentas were delivered, and Heather's had an odor which showed some signs of deterioration, which could have contributed to my elevated white blood cell count. Then Kevin's placenta was delivered. It wasn't until that moment we knew for sure that the placentas were not attached to each other.

Kevin Earl Tejan was born on February 13, 1988, at 4:41pm and was one pound and fifteen ounces and thirteen inches long. Bigger than Heather, but still very tiny. I felt pretty good after the delivery, and the family came in to say "hi," and then everyone disappeared on me to go see Kevin. He was doing well, and the doctor brought me pictures of him. Paul still hadn't come back to my room, and he was gone a long time visiting Kevin. I didn't think that was fair. However, it turns out that Kevin was born during Star Trek, one of Paul's favorite TV shows and he missed it that week. It happened to be on the TV in my room, and when Paul did return, he noticed that Star Trek was almost ending, and he had missed almost all of the show. I chuckled to myself and thought that was good payback since he got to visit Kevin first.

A few hours after Kevin was born, I got to sit up and walk to the bathroom for the first time in two and a half weeks. I was very wobbly. Then the nurse, Paul, and my mom helped me into a wheelchair, and they pushed me down the hall to see Kevin. He was so cute, and I fell in love with him instantly. He had a ventilator hood over him which provided oxygen. He was so active – he lifted up his little bottom and kicked his legs and moved his arms. He was so tiny but so adorable! I couldn't believe he was here, and thank you, Jesus, he was doing well. The nurse explained everything he was hooked up to, and I got to hold his tiny little hand. It was a short visit, because I wasn't used to sitting up, and was getting a little dizzy.

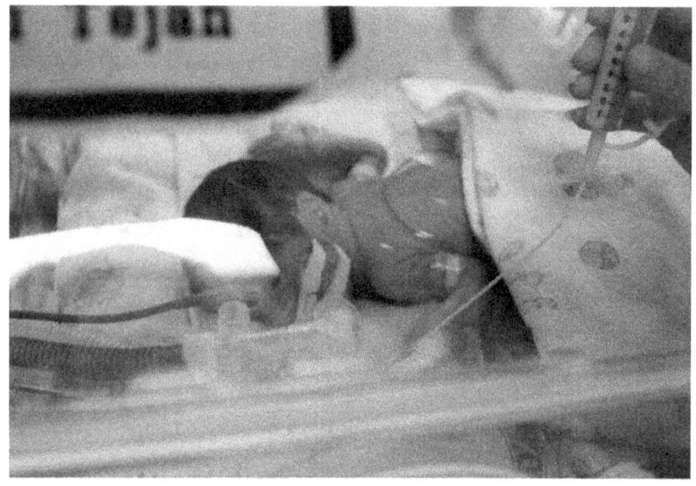

Kevin's first baby pictures

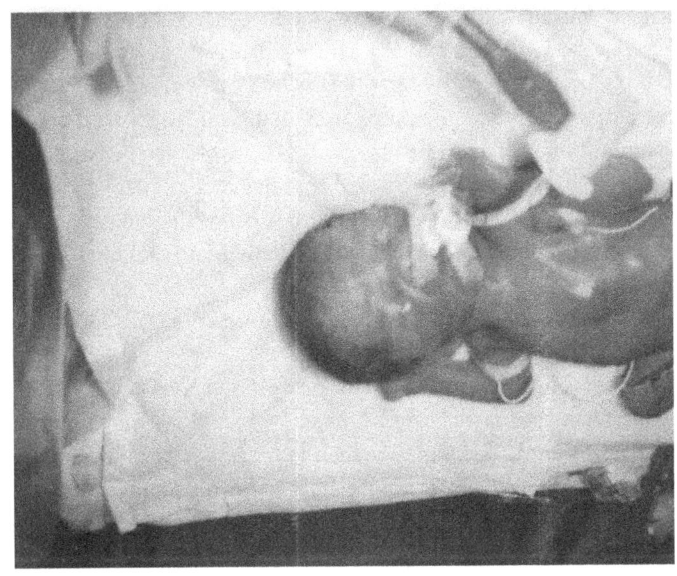

Kevin's first baby pictures

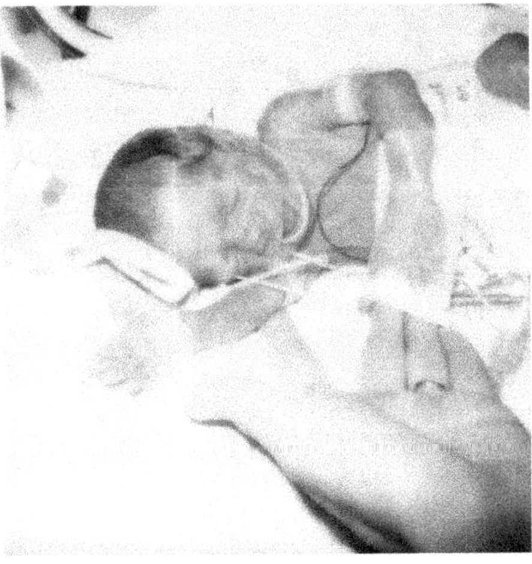

Kevin taken off of the ventilator at four days and doing well.

The next day after work, which happened to be Valentine's Day, Paul arrived at the hospital, and we went to see Kevin again. He was doing very well – still breathing room air, and the attending nurses decreased the oxygen volume to only fifteen breaths per minute; the rest he was doing on his own. Paul noticed that Kevin and he both slept the same way, as Kevin was asleep with his hand curled under and next to his face. We also noted that he had Paul's long toes. It was such a perfect day, just spending time looking at our beautiful son and marveling at all of the tiny details we had waited so long to see. My Mom and Stepdad, Darlene and Jack, came to visit again. They were so excited to see Kevin again! This time they brought me a present, a nursing gown, and an adorable stuffed animal for Kevin.

> *Diary note – 02/14/1988 – Mom gave me a nursing nightgown before she left the hospital that night. She intended on buying a nightgown for herself, but when she went to pay for it, the sales lady said it was for nursing. Mom hadn't seen anything like it before. She thought I could get some use out of it.*

The following day was a Monday, and Paul had to go back to work. I was still in the hospital, wondering how long I would be able to stay there with Kevin. I knew that he would be staying about three months, and I would be discharged soon and would have to come home without my baby. It was a day I was not looking forward to at all.

> *Diary note – 02/15/1988 – I woke up early the next morning and visited Kevin at 4:45 am and called Paul to give him an update before he had to leave for work. Kevin was doing fine and just as cute as ever. Later at 11:00 am I went back to see him again. They were going to take him off the ventilator and put him under an oxygen hood only. I held his little hand and comforted him when they took the intubation tube out of his throat. He didn't like that and cried. It couldn't have felt good.*

Later that same day the hospital discharged me, as the insurance company figured that my eighteen-day stay was long enough. When I found this out, I called Paul, and he left work early to come get me. I didn't want to leave Kevin, but I knew this day would have to come sometime. Now it was here, and I had to prepare myself to leave my tiny little baby. It was so nice to be able to walk down the hall and visit him, but now I would be half an hour away in Ontario and would be longing to see him every moment. Words can't express everything I was feeling as I prepared to leave. So much had happened since we had first arrived several weeks earlier.

One of the things you do when you know you are going to the hospital to deliver your baby is to "pack a bag" of clothes and whatever else you might need during your hospital stay. Well, I never got to do that step. I never prepared a bag, and in fact, to this day I've never seen a list of what you're supposed to pack in your bag. I can imagine it was clothes to wear home, toothbrush, toothpaste, hairbrush. I also missed my first Lamaze class that was supposed to be the night Heather was born. That means I missed all the instructions on how to give birth, how to push out a baby and what I should pack in my hospital bag. Now it was time for me to leave the hospital, and I didn't have any clean clothes to wear. I was there for three weeks, and it never occurred to me that I should ask Paul to bring some clothes for me to wear home.

Now what? I ended up putting on that baby blue nursing nightgown my mom had brought me and said to myself "This is so UGLY." It was just awful. It was huge and baggy and had these openings in the side for breastfeeding that looked like flaps that could open up and wave to a crowd of people. It was so embarrassing looking, but it was all I had to wear.

I was waiting for Paul to pick me up, but while he was driving home from work, he got into an accident. He was rear-ended on the freeway and then pushed into the car in front of him, and of course, the car that hit him took off, leaving Paul to be the responsible party in the accident. It was incredibly unfair, but it didn't end there. Paul continued on his way to the hospital to pick me up, and while driving down the road, the hood of the truck flew up. He was able to pull off the road quickly and not get into another accident that day. He was very lucky. What a day!

Finally, Paul arrived at the hospital, and we went to visit Kevin. The only thing I felt comfort in that day was the fact that I knew he was in good hands with the nurses, doctors, and their knowledge to make Kevin well, and I had to trust that they would do a better job than they did with Heather. There were life-altering mistakes made that shouldn't have happened at all.

As I think back on that day, I realize now I was so focused on Kevin that it didn't even cross my mind as to "where" Heather was. With Heather, my focus was on the fact that she had died, and even though I was miserable and in so much emotional pain, I had to hold onto my mental faculties for Kevin. It wasn't until I was home and received a phone call from Forest Lawn Mortuary that I knew her status. They said they were going to handle the funeral arrangements and they wanted to know when they could transfer her to their mortuary. I was so clueless, but I don't imagine anyone really knows the answers to those questions the first time they have to answer them. I had to ask "Where is she now?"

I was surprised to hear that she was still at the hospital morgue downstairs, refrigerated. I didn't expect to hear that she was still there, and I told the mortuary I would have to get back to them.

As Paul and I left the hospital that day, I realized that there was one more stop we had to make before getting home. The medical supply store was holding an electric breast pump for me. I felt that breastfeeding was the only thing I could do to help Kevin grow and get healthy enough to come home. The nurses and doctors were keeping him alive, and I was providing his food.

We arrived at the medical supply store, and I didn't want to get out of the truck. I didn't want anyone to see me in that baby blue nursing gown that was just floating on me and only went down to my calves. I felt ugly and looked so homely. I begged Paul to go into the store to get the pump for me, but he said, "I don't know what I'm supposed to get. How am I supposed to know what that thing looks like? I really need you to go with me." To be honest, I think we were both embarrassed. Talking about breastfeeding was uncomfortable for him, and the ugly nursing gown was embarrassing to me. We both ended up going into the medical supply store together and picked up the electric breast pump. It was $80 a month to rent, but I thought I'd try it out.

We arrived home about 5:30 p.m. that day. I had been away for so long; it felt good to be home. One thing that stood out to me, however, was that the house was so quiet. It wasn't what I expected it to be. I should have been bringing home our son and daughter to the beautiful nursery we had set up for them, but instead, I was walking inside without either of them with me. There isn't really a way to adequately explain what it's like, coming home without my son and knowing that even when we did bring him home, my daughter wouldn't be with us.

Before all of this tragedy happened, we had painted and wallpapered the nursery, and we had bought two cribs and placed them side by side in the room together. The nursery was so cute with bears and balloons and yellow, pink and blue colors. Walking back into that room and seeing the two cribs was very difficult. I cried, and my heart just felt shattered.

It just wasn't fair. No one should ever have to go through losing a child; it's painful and unnatural. I took some time to feel that still fresh sorrow washing over me, and then my protective instincts kicked in. I knew I had to stay strong and think about the future; Paul and I did still have our son who was fighting for his life and would come home when he was ready. He was only two days old, and as he had been born so early and so small, he had many hurdles to get over; it was going to be a long road. His health was still in danger and would be for a long time. I knew in my heart I had to be strong for him, for both of us.

Paul and I went out to dinner that night. We were so nervous being away from the phone that we stopped at Radio Shack to buy a beeper (yes, a beeper) so that the hospital could reach us at any time. We felt so relieved once we got it! That was a very high-tech device at the time in 1988. We had to write a procedure for the nurses on how to use it. Cell phones were about as big as a shoe box and very expensive. We spent a hundred dollars on a beeper and went right home and charged it up. During that time, there were answering machines on a loop to loop cassette tape. You still had to be present pushing the Play, Rewind and Stop buttons to hear the message. It sounds like the stone age now, almost thirty years later, but a beeper was cutting edge technology at that time. At least with that, we would have the freedom to leave the house, and if it went off, we could rush to any telephone to call back whoever was trying to get a hold of us.

Once we were home, we called the hospital for an update on Kevin, and he was doing great. In fact, they had taken him off of the oxygen hood, and he was breathing entirely on his own.

Diary note - 02/16/1988 - He is still breathing on his own with no oxygen hood. Later around 11:00am, he had his first apnea bradycardia – where babies go into a deep sleep and forget to breathe. He received some medicine for this and is just fine now. He had three apnea bradycardias from 11:00am – 5:00pm which the nurse said was ok and there wasn't anything to worry about.

Diary note - 02/17/1988 - Kevin is doing great. He has had only one apnea bradycardia and is showing off today. When the nurses walk into his room, he opens his eyes and yawns at them and looks all around the room. They say he is very cute.

Diary note - 02/18/1988 – 03/02/1988 (for two weeks) - Kevin's Brady's were increasing to an average of four a day, so they put him back on a CPAP machine (Continuous Positive Airway Pressure). This machine has tubes that were strapped to his face to apply pressure of oxygen going into his lungs and to stimulate him to not sleep so deeply.

The CPAP machine didn't look comfortable at all. It looked heavy and cumbersome attached to his tiny little face. I felt so bad for him lying there with all those tubes coming out of him. He wore it for two weeks, and he wasn't getting much better. Finally, the doctors decided to put him back on the ventilator. The Brady's weren't decreasing like the doctors wanted them to do, so they had to re-intubate him. This was Kevin's first real setback.

He had been doing so well, but his little body was tiring out. He needed to rest by not having to struggle to breathe. It was necessary to put him back on the ventilator. The oxygen settings were low, and the goal was to allow him to grow and rest and not have to expend so much energy to just breathe. It was just too taxing on him.

Although it was difficult to see him back on the ventilator and hooked up with more tubes coming out of his little body, we knew it was necessary. The doctors explained the reason for doing this, and it did make sense, so we just had to go along with it. Despite everything we'd gone through up to that point, despite losing our daughter, we knew that there had to be a trust relationship between us and the nurses and doctors, whether we liked it or not. Our motto had become "*In God we trust, and in Doctors, we ask questions.*" Knowledge is power, so we asked a lot of questions in order to understand the "why" behind what they were doing with our precious son on a daily basis.

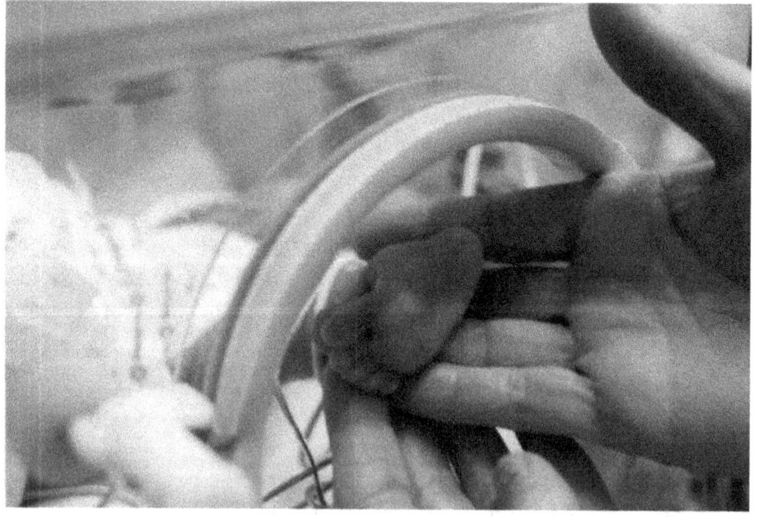

His tiny little foot

The next day the doctor explained they would be scanning his brain to see if there were any bleeds on his brain. That was worrisome because they caused

Heather to have a large bleed on her brain when they gave her too much fluids. Kevin's ultrasound of the head came back fine. Thank goodness he looked alright– no bleeding on the brain. He didn't like having the ultrasound and cried. They put a cold gel on his head for the ultrasound machine to pick up the inside of his head. I wouldn't want cold and gooey stuff rubbed on my head either; we felt very thankful and lucky that everything turned out to be fine.

Just when you think everything is going to be alright, then the nurses and doctors tell you something new that possibly could go wrong with his development. They only tell you little pieces of information as they see fit. They do this on purpose because they say that if they told us everything that could go wrong and what they were going to test for next, we would be too overwhelmed and nervous for our new little one all the time. First, it was the test to see if he had any bleed on his brain, then they checked his eyesight to see if he was blind. It was one thing after another and would be a long time before his tiny, young, little life would be out of danger.

We played with him for a while, and he yawned for us. He looked so cute yawning, but we took that as our cue for Paul and me to go home. Paul had been up since 6:00 a.m. working all day long. I knew he was tired.

On our way home from the hospital, our beeper went off. It really surprised us. We drove fast to the first telephone booth we could find. (And yes, telephone booths were everywhere in 1988; they hadn't disappeared yet from the street corners and gas stations.) Dr. Emery told us they found a very small opening in the Patent Ductus Arteriosus (PDA) from an X-ray they had done earlier, but thankfully they caught it early. They were looking for it since Heather had a history of this. In fact, Kevin was not even showing signs of a problem with this yet, but they purposely looked for the possibility of the problem. I think they were watching him extra close since they knew that we had lost Heather due to some hospital errors.

For this condition, they administered three doses of medication 24 hours apart, and this cleared up the problem. We were so thankful we had the beeper. It paid for itself the very first day with an incredible peace of mind.

I've been asked before if we ever thought of suing the hospital when we lost Heather.

Paul and I talked about the several errors they made, but to be honest, we were so stressed out with everything we had gone through, and our main focus was to get Kevin strong enough to come home with us. My dad was also a strong influence to not sue the hospital or my obstetrician. He didn't believe in suing and thought everyone in the world was sue happy, and that it was the wrong thing to do. How could we make waves at the hospital when we were depending on them to take good care of Kevin? We didn't want to take any chances with him not getting the best care he could have. Looking back on it, if we were more mature and strong and not as emotional, we might have pursued legal action, but it was just too much to think about or deal with at the time.

Every day after, when Paul got off of work, we would drive almost twenty-two miles from Ontario to Loma Linda to visit Kevin. One day Paul had already driven one hundred thirty miles to and from Pasadena, but we couldn't wait to see Kevin again. To us, that was just a normal thing to do; to visit your child who was in the hospital. One day one, a nurse told us that some parents didn't visit more than once a week or every two weeks, and some didn't visit at all. We were shocked! We were fortunate to live only twenty-two miles from where Kevin was being cared for. The nurses also said that the babies that were visited and talked to and touched more often recovered quicker and better. That made perfect sense to us, and we wanted to be there. It was the best part of our day.

I remember one day thinking about driving to the hospital on my own so that I could spend the entire day with Kevin. I never did, because I thought that would be unfair to Paul, so I waited until he came home, and we always went together. I also went back to work after six weeks of maternity leave. It was good for me to get back into a routine and dive back into my work. Being at my job would help my days to go faster until we could go see Kevin again, and there just wasn't anything left for me to do at home. The nursery was ready for Kevin; the house was clean, the laundry finished, the grocery shopping was done, dinners were prepared and in the freezer. All I was doing was waiting for Paul to come home from work so we could visit our precious little boy.

Walking back into the office was familiar and strange all at once. I figured that everyone there knew what happened to Heather and Kevin, but I didn't know exactly what they knew. Many came up to me and said they were happy to see me again. They felt bad for everything I had gone through, and they were there for me if I wanted to talk, or cry, or just needed a friend. I remember my boss just shaking his head and looking at me and said, "If there is anything you need, just let me know." He said that he couldn't imagine everything Paul and I had been through, and he was there to help. It was comforting to be able to go back into a work environment where I felt so supported by my co-workers.

I took the electric breast pump with me every day so that I could pump at lunch time. I tried it for a few days but wasn't very successful; I was just too nervous that someone was going to walk in on me. One day I thought I could get away without using it, but that turned out to be such a mistake! It was painful not pumping in the middle of the day, and I ended up in tears and went to my boss and said that I had to quit my job. I needed to do this for Kevin. It was the only thing that I could give him to help him gain weight and come home to us. He said to not worry and said that if I wanted to take a longer lunch, that would be fine. I told him that that would definitely help the situation, as I would be able to drive home to pump, which was only about five miles away from work. My boss was so understanding about the situation and made me feel as if I were a valued employee. I appreciated him so much. I remained at my job there for the next three months, until it was time for Kevin to be released from the hospital.

I kept myself busy until then by focusing on my work. It helped me a little bit, so that I didn't focus on losing Heather twenty-four hours a day and seven days a week and did my best to keep my focus on getting to the end of the day when we would go visit Kevin. After I had returned to work, Paul and I kept up this same routine and would visit Kevin daily. It was a difficult schedule, and we were so tired that we ate in a lot of restaurants after visiting him. I had food prepared and stored in the freezer but was too tired to microwave it at 9 or 10 o'clock at night. It was just easier to stop at a restaurant. Once we got home, I had to use the electric breast pump before going to sleep. It was a grueling schedule for three months that we kept up every night, except for one night when Paul thought he was coming down with a cold, so we skipped that one night...one night in three months. I'm so glad we did it that way. It was worth it all. Something fun and exciting happened every night we visited him. We just couldn't wait until we could bring him home.

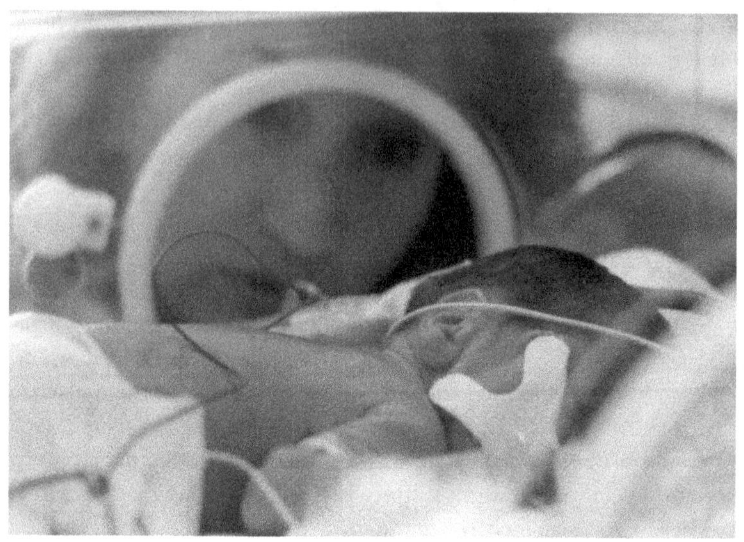

Joyce gazing into Kevin's incubator.

BABY GO TO SLEEP TAPE SYSTEM

Kevin was around three weeks old, and Paul wanted to find something that would help Kevin to thrive better; something he could do for his son. He felt helpless just watching him lay there in his little incubator. He needed to gain weight and get healthy if he was ever to go home with us. Paul was very good at coming up with ideas to solve a problem, and he enjoyed researching things. One day he discovered an audio tape system to help a baby stay calm. It was called "Baby Go to Sleep" by Terry Woodford. He contacted the company and explained what Kevin was going through and how he had had a rough start to his life and wondered if their system could help Kevin. They explained how their system worked and said they not only thought it would be helpful to him, but their company wanted to help. They sent Paul a tape with the speakers to put in his incubator after hearing about our tiny premature baby who was struggling for his life.

Paul and I brought in a radio/tape recorder to attach to the speakers and play this special tape. We put the speakers inside Kevin's incubator, and they played the music very slowly and calmly. There was a mother's heartbeat playing softly in the background as well to mimic being in the womb. The nurses were really surprised to see this device we brought in, as they hadn't heard of it before, but they thought it was a great idea! Kevin was resting on his waterbed, listening to soft music and mommy's heartbeat, gaining weight, and getting healthy to come home to us. It was a wonderful device that could help in many situations even after bringing baby home. We never used it after Kevin came home, but now when I think back on it, it was a great idea to help quiet a fussy baby. I looked on the internet years later to see if the company was still in business, and it was. This same tape that came out in 1987 can still be purchased online today. Incredible! It helped us, and it's nice to see that almost thirty years later, it's still out there helping other parents today.

Diary note - 03/05/1988 – Saturday (three weeks old now) - Today they started feeding him breast milk. He is tolerating it just fine. Since he has been re-intubated, he hasn't had any Brady's. It seems that's what he needed. His body needed a break so he could grow. Today he is 900 grams or 2 pounds (He's gained only one ounce in three weeks).

Diary note - 03/06/1988 - Doing just fine. Kevin's milk was increased from 3cc's to 4cc's.

BABY BOTTLE ORGANIZER

Kevin was so little, and his dad wanted to do even more for him. Paul was always engineering something or changing something to make it better. That's the kind of super dad he is. While visiting Kevin one day, we heard the nurse tell another nurse that she needed more bottles of milk for Kevin and asked her to bring some of his milk from the refrigerator where they stored all the mom's milk. We offered to get the milk for her. Paul and I went down the hall to bring back the milk to the nurses. That's when we discovered the nurses grabbed any of his bottles with his name on it, and that it wasn't always the oldest bottle that was expressed first. You may have heard of FIFO...First in, first out! Well, that wasn't happening. We wanted him to have the freshest milk first in the order it was expressed. Paul said he had to fix that situation right away. The wheels in his engineering mind started to turn. His son wasn't getting the milk in the right order, even though the bottles were labeled and dated; the nurses were always in a hurry and didn't usually look at the dates when expressed. We delivered the bottles of milk to the nurse and went home for the evening.

The next day, Paul designed a Baby Bottle Organizer. This contraption worked sort of how a soda machine works. You load the bottles of milk at the top, and they roll down to the bottom. He created a system that allowed the bottles Kevin needed to roll out in the correct order - it was genius! He made this out of sheet metal and brought it to the nurses to show them that Kevin's milk would now be in this milk organizer and they would always have his milk in date order. They were so impressed with this new organizer! Kevin's milk bottles would never get mixed up again. The nurses liked the fact that we were parents who were so involved in our son's well-being. We just wanted to help as much as we could. It's all that we could do at the time.

Diary note - 03/07/1988 - Kevin is now getting 5cc's of milk every three hours and has grown to 960 grams or two pounds and two ounces. Now he has gained three ounces since birth, and it's been three and a half weeks.

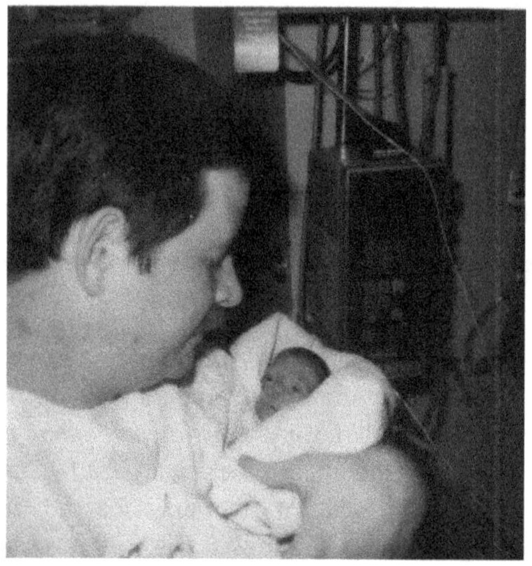

Paul holding Kevin

Diary note - 03/08/1988 - He received a blood transfusion today. (Daddy's blood). Paul was able to be a direct donor to Kevin. It was such a good thing to be able to donate directly with the AIDS epidemic and problems with the blood supply around this time.   He is now two pounds four ounces.

A BIG EVENT–MOVING UPSTAIRS

Kevin had become stronger and healthier; enough to move him from the intensive care unit, upstairs to the department where babies are on their way to going home. It was like getting a promotion! We were so happy, and it was a nice surprise for us that night. However, they never told us they were moving him. When we went to visit him in his normal hospital room, he wasn't there. It was completely disturbing, and I remember asking "Oh my God, where is Kevin?" Thankfully, the nurses said he was doing great. He was, in fact, doing so well that they moved him to a different unit where the care level is less intensive because he was getting so much healthier. I just wish they had told us before we had arrived at the hospital that evening. He also had his first bath during this time, but I don't think he enjoyed it too much!

Kevin now had a window in his room, and he looked very comfortable resting in his new little isolate. I guess the window was more for the parents and nurses because Kevin certainly couldn't see out the window or see the view of the mountains. This room was much quieter and more peaceful, with only a couple of alarms going off once in a while. It was a relief to see him resting much better. In the other NICU, he would jerk or make a face when the alarms went off. If you have ever stayed overnight in the hospital, you know how hard it is to rest there. It's the same for the young and the old.

Diary note – 03/22/1988 – Kevin looks great. Even the nurses say he is a cute baby. He is looking more babyish each day now since he is gaining weight and gaining some baby fat. The hospital gave him his first T-shirt to wear. Previously the nurses didn't want any clothes on him so they could see his chest and watch him breathe. He is now two pounds and 14 ounces, and we will soon be able to hold him without the tubes and wires all connected. Maybe in two more weeks.

Diary note - 03/23/1988 - Kevin looks great! He is resting very well, so well that he didn't want to wake up for us, but he held our finger as we enjoyed watching him sleep.

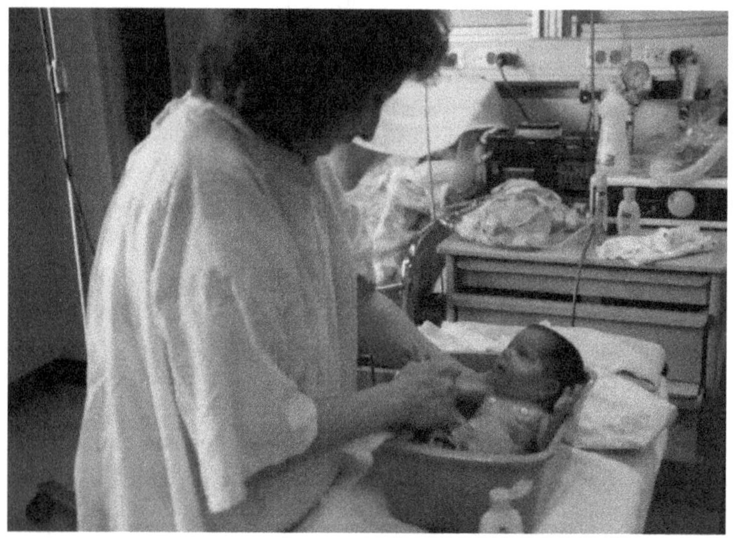

Kevin looks like he is enjoying his tub bath.

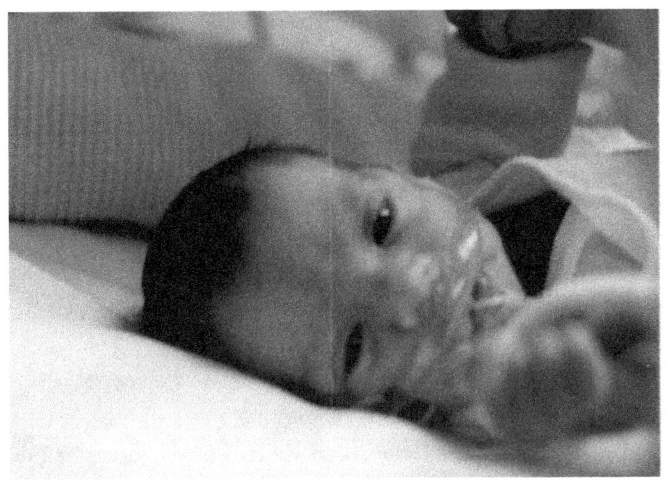

Kevin looking cute and getting a little baby fat on him.

HOSPITAL ADVENTURES

One night after leaving the hospital we needed to fill up the car with gas. We stopped at the gas station closest to the freeway like we had done many nights previously. Back then you always had to go inside and pay before pumping gas, paying at the pump wasn't an option yet. We were driving an older white Cadillac, and as I went inside to pay, Paul was getting the hose in the tank, when all of a sudden, some stranger jumped into the driver's seat! Before we could do anything, the man was driving away in our car. Paul was running behind the car and yelling at him to stop and was banging on the back of the trunk. Talk about a gutsy thief, stealing our car right in front of us; and it was dangerous for Paul, too. What if that guy had had a gun? We watched this creep drive off with our car down the road and onto the freeway. We just stood there; there wasn't anything we could do except call 911. We were in complete shock. We got in touch with the police right away and gave them a description of what this man looked like, as well as the make and model of our car. Nothing special, but special enough for someone to steal it. We bought it when I was pregnant for $3,000 from a private party. We just wanted a car that was big and safe and not too expensive, because we couldn't afford any car payments.

I can't remember how we got home that night. We must have called a friend to come and pick us up. About three weeks later we got a call from the insurance company, telling us that they had found our car. It had been used in a robbery to steal beer from a convenience store in Redlands. What's funny, is that when the thieves stole a six-pack of beer at a convenience store and went to drive away, the car battery died and they were caught, and our car was recovered. It was at an impound yard about a half hour away from the hospital. We drove to the impound yard that night and had to pay a fee of a couple of hundred dollars to get our car back, which just felt insane - here we were robbed of our car right in front of us, and we had to pay to get it back. When we got back into our car, we looked in the glove compartment to make sure all of the proper paperwork was still there. What surprised us when we opened it was that, apparently, the thieves had used our car to go to church. Inside the compartment was a church bulletin and a Bible. I guess church didn't help them that particular week though, because they were caught robbing a store. It was also incredibly frustrating to see that they had messed up our car badly. It was really hard to get it started, and when Paul finally did, the brakes barely worked. We were lucky to be able to drive it home and get there in one piece. It was just such a mess. The upholstery was dirty and torn; it needed a new battery and brakes, and a bunch of other things. We eventually got it fixed it up and made it look nice, and it was drivable again.

It was a couple of months later that we went outside to get into the car and go somewhere, I think to a hardware store. Normally, we parked it in the garage or our driveway, but this time it was parked on the street. As soon as we walked up to the car, we found that someone else had broken into it again, and the lock steering assembly was broken. I guess that someone or something must have scared them off, or possibly our barking dogs. What was up with this old Cadillac? It wasn't that big of a deal as far as a vehicle goes, but it was sure popular with thieves. We ended up fixing the lock and steering column assembly and put the car up for sale. We had had enough of having to repair the car.

Diary note - 03/28/1988 - I got a call from the hospital. They said they ran out of Human Milk Fortifier. I couldn't believe that a big hospital could run out of such an important product for babies.

Another opportunity for Paul to help Kevin - Loma Linda University Medical Center, a leading hospital in the care for preemies, ran out of Human Milk Fortifier, which their preemie babies needed this to help them grow and gain weight. It's hard to believe this could happen, but it did. The fortifier was a powder that was added to either baby formula or breast milk for added nutrients and calories in the babies' diet. It's sort of like having a loaded milkshake with lots of extra calories and vitamins in it.

I called Paul at work to tell him what had happened, and he immediately started calling around to other hospitals to see if he could locate it. That was a big deal for Paul to pick up a phone. Talking on the phone was his least favorite thing to do in life, but my husband had a mission! It was another research project for him to help provide for his son. Soon enough, Paul was able to locate it at Pomona Valley Hospital. He told them he was calling for Loma Linda University Medical Center, and that they had run out of the Human Milk Fortifier for their babies. The

Pomona Valley Hospital said they had it available, and it was no problem for him to come and pick it up. It was amazing! Pomona Hospital was about twenty minutes from our home in Ontario. In fact, Paul passed by the hospital every day coming and going to work. He rushed over to the hospital, and they gave him two-hundred packs of the Human Milk Fortifier we so desperately needed. He was so thankful to the hospital staff! They were incredibly kind and didn't question him at all. They just gave it to him, and Paul delivered it to Loma Linda Hospital. The nurses were so happy to see that Paul located it, not to mention surprised.

I don't think they ever thought that a parent would show up with Human Milk Fortifier, but they didn't know Paul, his tenacity or his research abilities. The nurses said they would set it aside for Kevin, but we told them to give it to all of the babies who needed it. It was for everyone, not just Kevin. They were surprised that we would want to share something so important to the growth of our baby, but we wanted other babies to have it too. All of the babies in the NICU were just as important as Kevin and were also struggling. They needed the help just as much as he did. Kevin's nurses said that he would have his first, but they would share it with the other babies as well, which was fine with us.

Diary note – 3/29/1988 – I tried breastfeeding Kevin for the first time today. The nurses wanted to see if he was almost ready to be bottle fed. He is 33 weeks now and 3 pounds 3 ounces. He needs to be at least 4 1/2 pounds before he can go home. Hurry up, Kevin, grow some more.

Diary note – 3/30/1988 – He looks great today. Getting a little chubby at 3 lbs 4 oz.

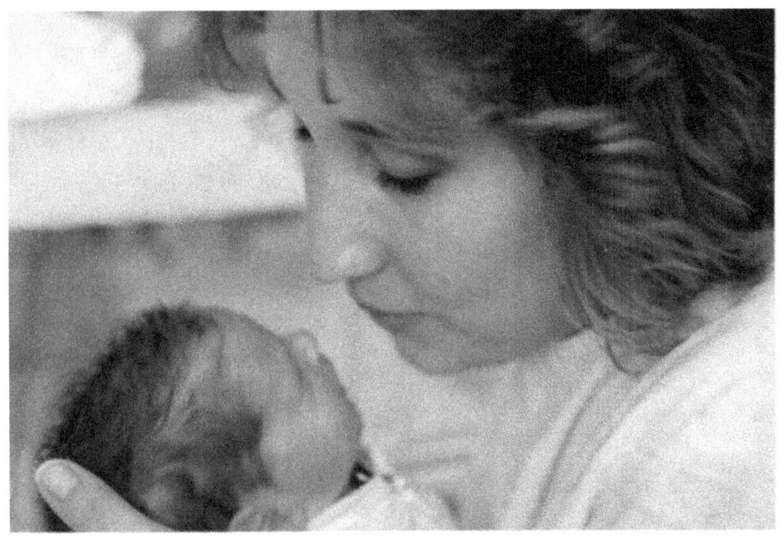

I adore him so.

Paul holding Kevin while he sleeps on his chest.

Diary note - 4/1/1988 - 3lbs 5 oz – 1520 grams. Kevin finally weighs enough so we can take him out of the crib each night and hold him. Grandma Neubauer, my mom, saw Kevin this afternoon and she held Kevin for the first "official" time.

Diary note - 4/2/1988 – It's Saturday – Uncle Larry visited Kevin today, and all three of us (Paul, Joyce, and Larry) took turns holding him. We took lots of pictures. I dressed him in his first outfit from Grandma Neubauer. It was fun.

Diary note - 4/3/1988 – Easter Sunday – I put his Easter outfit on him today, and it swam on him. It was a "preemie size" outfit, but it was still too big. He is still so tiny. Maybe it will fit by the time he gets to come home. It's an adorable light blue onesie with his name embroidered on it.

Diary note - 4/6/1988 – We held Kevin and videotaped him. Today he was bottle fed at 7:00 pm by his nurse. She gave him 5cc's of milk, and at 10:00 pm we fed him 15cc's.

Diary note - 4/7/1988 – Thursday – I fed him ½ of his feeding by bottle. He's getting so big now – 3lbs 12oz. He is very alert and doing well. Although they did increase his Somophyllin level because of a couple Brady's that day. Somophyllin is supposed to help him breathe easier.

Diary note - 4/8/1988 – Friday – I fed him again, and he took ½ his feeding. He coughed a couple of times, but that's o.k. He is learning to suck, swallow and breathe all at the same time, as well as mommy learning how to feed and burp him and read his face as to when he has had enough to eat and needs to rest or burp. As of now, he is a quiet burper, and it's hard to tell when or if he burped.

Diary note - 4/9/1988 – Paul thought he might be coming down with a cold, so we skipped seeing Kevin today. It was the only night we had missed out of two months of his new little life. We miss him so much. We can't wait to see him tomorrow. If Paul is truly sick, I think I'll go to the hospital by myself.

Diary note - 4/9 /1988 - Our neighbor, Kim, brought Kevin a big bag of clothes today - lots of t-shirts and sleeping gowns that her baby Ashley had outgrown. That was so sweet of her.

Diary note - 4/12/1988 - Tonight Daddy bottle fed him for the first time. He is two months old.

One night not long after, Kevin was halfway through his bottle feeding, and he stopped sucking and got lazy. He was just looking around. He was quite alert but wasn't interested in eating. Kevin had to eat! He had to eat so he could eventually come home with us. I remember this so clearly. Paul was determined to have Kevin finish his bottle. So, Paul squeezed the bottle a little extra and made him eat. He pushed his little cheeks together so he would swallow. Eventually, Kevin finished the whole bottle, which was a relief. It may sound like a small thing now but seeing your three-pound baby fighting for its life make you truly realize how those moments were actually some of the big ones. Those hurdles we jumped over as a family gave us the drive to conquer the next ones, and the next. I think it was also a really special bonding experience for the two of them, and they did a good job together, Kevin and Daddy.

Later that night we were able to give Kevin a bath. It was a fun night, caring for him as if we were already at home. The nurse gave us a little basin to bathe him in; you know the kind that holds about two gallons of water; the kind that the nurse gives you if you need to throw up. I shampooed Kevin's hair and washed him clean, but it was hard to tell if he enjoyed it or not. It was probably scary to him, but he was very good and didn't even cry. Then I dried him off and put lotion on him and dressed him. It was a lot of fun. I couldn't wait until we were able to bring him home.   His bath was the first time I held him naked without any wires or tubes hooked to him. It was great and just felt so natural.

Diary note - 4/14/1988 - Kevin brady'ed (apnea bradycardia event) on me after feeding him.

Diary note - 4/15/1988 - Kevin brady'ed on me after feeding him.

Diary note - 4/16/1988 – Two and a half months old now. Kevin took his whole feeding by bottle again. (40cc's – 1 3/4 oz.). He was alert and sucking well. Today Paul and I went to Toys R Us and bought a diaper bag, shampoo items, and a new pacifier that squeaks. He wasn't very interested in it because he was sleepy. The night nurse weighed him, and he gained 90 grams (3 oz.). Now he is 2000 grams (4 1/2 pounds). He could technically go home now, but he is still having brady's. He has to go ten days without brady's before he can go home. Today NO brady's...just nine more days to go. Yea!!

Diary note - 4/18/1988 – Monday - Kevin pulled his feeding tube out of his mouth for the last time. He rebelled and decided that from now on he was going to take the whole bottle without a feeding tube. He had enough with feeding tubes. Then he brady'ed while Paul was feeding him.

Diary note - 4/19/1988 – Tuesday - I gave him a sponge bath while Paul took pictures and Kevin sucked his thumb. He was really hungry since he gets fed every four hours now. Paul fed him this time, but it wasn't easy this time. He had three brady's and needed oxygen to recover. We had never seen him have so much trouble recovering from a brady. It was very scary. Paul said he was going to get shipped to the "brat ward" if he didn't do better the next time. The nurse said that she felt he was just so hungry that he sucked too fast without breathing. He just forgot. Soon he will have it all coordinated. Someday it should just "click" for him.

Diary note - 4/20/1988 – Wednesday - Tonight I shampooed his hair and gave him a tub bath. He didn't seem to mind too much. Then I fed him, and he had three mild Brady's on me, so I let his nurse, Reggie, finish the feeding. His heart rate also dropped on her so she rubbed his back and his heart rate came up again. He is now 4 pounds 9 1/2 oz.

Diary note - 4/21/1988 – Thursday - Today I got a call from Dennis at KIIS FM. They received the letter we sent, asking for a limo ride home from the hospital for Kevin. They granted our wish! How exciting! It was Paul's idea to write Rick Dees, KIIS FM, and tell him our story about the car getting stolen from one of our visits to see Kevin. So, we did. The letter was written as if Kevin was writing it from his incubator. We were so excited to have him come home from the hospital in a limo. Neither of us had ever ridden in a limo before.

Diary note - 4/22/1988 – Friday - Grandma Neubauer visited Kevin today. She helped with Kevin's tub bath, and then I fed him. He did o.k., only one mild brady. Grandma held him, and he had a brady on her. Then he was acting cute and smiling and reaching out his arms. Tonight, he cried for one of the first times. Doctors are testing him for a Rotavirus. I hope he doesn't have it.

Diary note - 4/23/1988 – Saturday - Today Paul spoke with Dr. Fargo. We were concerned about Kevin being near the other baby who had the Rotavirus. We didn't want the same nurse caring for Kevin and the other baby at the same time. It just was too easy to goof and not wash their hands before touching Kevin.

Dr. Fargo also thought my milk might be bothering him because this last week he has been fussy. The only thing different about my diet is we have gone out to dinner after seeing him, and I had decaf coffee. So, I have now cut that out of my diet. I think he was coming down with the Rotavirus and didn't feel well and no one knew it yet.

Diary note - 4/24/1988 – Sunday - Dr. Fargo called today. She said Kevin tested positive for the Rotavirus. He should be over it in a week at the latest. We were upset to hear this, but she said it wouldn't delay his coming home. She also said she was working on getting him home by Friday. We can't wait! We just have to be trained on the apnea monitor, and they will release him to us. Now we know that it wasn't my milk that was making him fussy. It was the Rotavirus.

Diary note - 4/25/1988 – Monday - Today we spoke with the insurance company and made arrangements to be trained on the apnea bradycardia monitor. They will also provide a public health nurse to come to our house every so often to check on Kevin and answer any questions we had.

Diary note - 4/26/1988 – Tuesday - Dr. Fargo called today at work. They fed Kevin milk again, but it went right through him with real runny stools. Now he needed an IV for 3-4 days. Unfortunately, this will delay his coming home for at least a week.

Diary note - 4/27/1988 – Wednesday - Kevin had his eye test today, and he did great. His eyes are very good says the Ophthalmologist. He is up to 4 lbs 13 oz now. He weighs enough to come home, but because of catching that Rotavirus, he can't come home yet. Another setback.

Diary note - 4/29/1988 – Friday - Grandma and Grandpa Neubauer came to visit Kevin again tonight. Grandpa had a cold, so he wore a mask and Grandma held him. She says that she can't wait until she can hold him at her house.

Diary note - 4/30/1988 – Saturday - Kevin is now 5 pounds today and doing well. Soon they will decrease the fluids in his IV and increase his milk intake. He is on his way to recovery and on his way home again.

Diary note - 5/3/1988 – Tuesday - Today Kevin has graduated from Preemie diapers to size Small diapers. He is 5 lbs 2 oz and doing well. He needs another blood transfusion again because he is a little anemic. The blood Paul donated in March has expired so he has to donate again for the third time, so the blood bank gave him a free t-shirt.

Diary note - 5/4/1988 – Wednesday - We spoke with Dr. Fargo today. She says Kevin might get to come home on Sunday, Mother's Day. Wouldn't that be the best Mother's Day gift ever! Friday, she will be able to let us know if he will be ready. He is now Rotavirus negative, and we don't have to wear gloves and isolation gowns around him. Kevin is up to 5 lbs. 3 oz.

The next night that we saw him, he looked great! He got his bath and was looking at Paul and I each time we spoke. He was very alert. He was given Pedialyte earlier in the day to help relax his intestines, and the following day the plan was to go back to him having breast milk. His nurse, Reggie, trained us more on how to care for him, and we signed a paper saying we understood and felt comfortable taking care of him. Kevin slept so cute and soundly that night. I didn't want to leave him. The following day was my last day at work, and I was so excited to take care of him full time!

Diary note - 5/8/1988 – Sunday - Kevin comes home today! Finally! It's been three long months. He came home with an Apnea bradycardia machine because of his history of stopping breathing

* * *

April 17, 1988

Rick Dees
KIIS FM Radio
6255 Sunset Blvd., Suite 1117
Los Angeles, California 90028

Dear Mr. Dees:

Hi, my name is Kevin Earl Tejan and I am 8 ½ weeks old. My Mommy and Daddy and I are 2 ½ of your 7 listeners. I was born early at 27 weeks at only 1 lb. 15 oz. and 13" long at Loma Linda University Medical Center. In my incubator I have a special bed with a speaker and under my mattress a transducer so I can hear and feel the vibrations of the music. This helps me to relax and grow strong so I can come home.

One night after my parents came to visit me, their car was stolen from the hospital. This truly came at a bad time because now I am ready to come home from the hospital for the very first time. When I was only 1 week old my daddy promised me a ride home in a stretch limousine so I could come home in style, but now that they lost their car, they are just like you Uncle Rick, they have no budget, and I was wondering Uncle Rick if you could help me out? I am coming home around April 24th. I would really be happy and so would my parents.
My nurses and I are all looking forward to hearing from you. Thank you very much.

Kevin Tejan

<u>Background</u>
Once upon a time we found out that we could not have children and we could not accept this concept so we found a special doctor that specializes in infertility. he discovered a process known as GIFT (Gamete Intra Fallopian Transfer). We were finally accepted into this program and had surgery to implant three eggs and sperm into the fallopian tubes.

Two weeks later we found out that we were going to have twins. A great deal of excitement was generated by many friends, family and co-workers at the Jet Propulsion Laboratory and Domino's Pizza Distribution Corp. Everyone knew of the importance of this very special gift we received. Unfortunately, premature labor came upon us and we had to give birth to a little girl (Heather) at 25 weeks into the pregnancy and she lived only two short days but was able to keep the boy (Kevin) inside for another eleven days, which I might add has only been done two other times in eleven years' time frame at Loma Linda. We believe that this has saved Kevin's life giving him that extra time in the womb. The hospital has worked very hard to try to save our little boy, especially under these circumstances. We are so happy he is doing well and we are looking forward to having him home very soon.

Paul and Joyce Tejan
Ontario, CA 91764

HOMECOMING AT LAST

The day had finally come. The day we got to bring Kevin home from a very long stay in the hospital. We were up early and were so excited to start the day! I called the phone number of the limo company that the radio station told us to contact. The limo driver who answered the phone sounded like he was asleep, and he was! It's a good thing I followed up and called him. He said he would be there within the hour but waiting felt like an eternity, so to kill time we gathered the video camera, car seat, diaper bag, etc. to take with us to pick up Kevin. The limo driver arrived, and we made our way to Loma Linda University Medical Center to pick up our son, to bring him home with us at long last.

My brother went with us to the hospital so that he could video tape everything happening that day. As soon as we arrived at the hospital, we went upstairs to get Kevin. First, I dressed him in his little blue preemie outfit with his name embroidered on it. It was big on him, but he still looked great! Then we said our goodbyes to the nurses and doctors before getting into the limo to go home. It was a fun drive, but it didn't seem real. There was champagne, and we celebrated with a glass, of course! Neither Paul or I had ever been in a limo, and obviously it was Kevin's first for everything. At one point in the hospital, Paul had promised Kevin a hamburger from In-N-Out Burger when he was able to come home, if he would eat and gain weight. To our shock and joy, the limo driver went through the drive-thru line for us. It was so much fun! I felt a bit silly going through the drive-thru in this big limo, but I was too excited to really think much of it. I was mostly just hoping that the driver could make the sharp turn, and not get stuck in the narrow driveway. He made it just fine, and we came home with two cheeseburgers and fries. It was the best homecoming celebration I could have asked for.

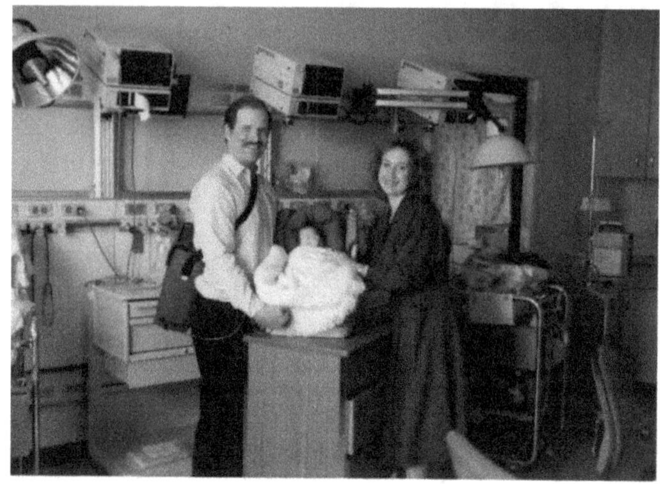

Kevin is ready to leave the hospital

Leaving the hospital in our first limo ride

Neighbors greet us at home

When the limo pulled up to our house, some of our family and neighbors were standing there waiting for us to arrive. They were so happy to finally meet Kevin! Everyone was waiting to see him, and we were equally excited to show him off. My Mom was calling him the Prince of Ontario and said we were already spoiling him. Well of course we were, and he deserved it! We had moved the second crib out of the nursery to downstairs into the family room. It was a great central place to take care of him. We put Kevin into his crib to settle in. He looked so tiny in his bed. He was a big five and a half pounds now. That's a long way from one pound fifteen ounces! What a major accomplishment. Kevin's homecoming was the very best day, celebrating with family, friends, and neighbors. Everyone had waited for three long months to see Kevin come home. I know they were worried about us and everything we had gone through, and I'm sure they were just as relieved as we were when he finally came home.

One month later, Paul's parents flew out from Florida to see their newest grandson. They came out not just to see their grandson for the first time, but it was also because of a request we had made to Paul's father, Claude, who had been a Lutheran Pastor for over fifty years. We had asked him if he would baptize our son, and he said that he would be delighted. Claude baptized him at the church where Paul and I were married several years earlier, and following the baptism, we shared a huge celebratory lunch with all of our family. It was an incredibly special day.

Kevin baptized by his Grandfather Claude Tejan

Grand-parents and Great-grand-parents celebrating afterward for lunch.

We knew Kevin would be coming home from the hospital with a bradycardia monitor and we wanted him to have it! We were willing to take every precaution possible to ensure our little boy was protected when we finally got to have him at home with us. It gave us a huge peace of mind having the monitor. We had two Shelties and one Maltese, and we taught them to run upstairs and jump on the crib to startle Kevin when his monitor started beeping. The monitor would start beeping, and the dogs would run to where Kevin was and bark and jump at the crib. It worked too! It was just enough stimulation to startle Kevin that it brought him out of his deep sleep and slowed his breathing. The dogs were much faster than we were, and they were also able to run upstairs to his crib much faster than we ever could.

Kevin experienced a history of apnea bradycardia events for over a year, and it was a huge comfort to us to have that extra help of the monitor. Knowing that we could all sleep safely was such a comfort, not to mention that if he slept too deeply, the monitor would go off and wake us all up. It is so devastating to lose a child, and we had already gone through so much with Kevin and Heather that we were determined to do all we could to keep our son safe. The apnea bradycardia monitor was a godsend to us.

Kevin seemed to Brady more often when he was eating. It takes a lot of coordination to suck on a bottle, swallow, and breathe all at the same time. The nurses said it would just take a while before he mastered it. When he was dozing off, he would brady, or when sleeping quietly and calmly, he would brady because he was in a deeper sleep. He would also have an episode when he cried or was overly tired or stressed. Paul and I were always doing something around the house and would either need to go to Home Depot or the grocery store or eat out at a restaurant. We definitely began to notice a correlation between having a long day with a lot of running around town and having many brady events that day. Once we recognized that, we limited our visits in a day and slowed down. It did make a difference for Kevin. His little body would get overstimulated, and it was too much activity for him.

We had the monitor for almost eighteen months, and probably could have given it back after a year, but we wanted that peace of mind, knowing that he was really out of the woods with having Brady's. Since he had so many of them for so long, we were afraid to let go of it. After a while, the monitor went off less and less, and we finally felt that it was ok to stop using it.

PART TWO: WALKING THROUGH THE VALLEY

DEVELOPMENTAL MILESTONES MET OR NOT MET

Having a premature baby can be scary. There are more risks for things to go wrong, and the doctors don't tell you everything that might go wrong, because it's just too much to absorb and comprehend if you hear it all at once. All you know is that you have a tiny baby that needs you, that needs a lot of love and support to grow up. Doctors give a premature infant a corrected age to adjust for keeping track of milestones that are normally met. For instance, a one-year-old baby might walk on his birthday, where a one-year-old baby who was born prematurely by three months has a corrected age of nine months. You wouldn't expect things from a nine-month-old that a one-year-old could do. By the time your baby is about two years old, they have caught up with what a two-year-old would be doing normally as far as developmental milestone markers. That's how you view the development of a preemie.

For instance, someone you don't know may come up to you at the grocery store and ask you how old your baby is. You can say either nine months or one year, it's your choice, and it also depends on how much explaining you want to do or how much time you have to fill in the details. If you said one year, then the predictable thing they ask is "Is he walking yet"? If you answer "No" then they say "well *my* child walked at ten months, blah, blah, blah." You know how people react. They love to compare what their baby was doing at one-year-old, and you can't make an exact comparison if you have a preemie. I found it was easier to just say the corrected age and not have to explain so much at certain times. Now if I was sitting in a park enjoying the day and relaxing and wanted to make small talk with other parents; for me, that was a more reasonable time to talk about our babies and what exciting new developments happened that week.

Kevin was meeting all of his corrected age milestones up until the age of nine months. The hospital had a follow-up program for all of their NICU babies, and it was time for his nine-month NICU follow up appointment. I remember the events of this particular check-up so clearly. The doctor was moving Kevin's legs and arms, evaluating him, and although everything looked normal to me, but the doctor was concerned about one side. I can't remember which side it actually was, but he noticed a weakness on one side of Kevin's body and thought it might be a possible problem. I felt dread course through me, hearing myself ask out loud "What it is?" Kevin's doctor said that maybe it was Cerebral Palsy, but he wasn't sure. Kevin would hold his foot a little differently when putting weight on it, and it seemed weaker than the other side. His doctor said, "Don't worry about it now, because it might just work itself out and become a non-issue." That's what I hoped for, and three months later when they re-evaluated him everything actually looked good! Kevin had equal strength on both sides of his body.

THE EARLY YEARS

Our son was such a good baby, and he had such a sweet temperament nearly all the time - until we took him to a restaurant, that is. That's when he threw a fit. I can't count the number of restaurants we walked out of because he would just cry uncontrollably, and nothing we did there would be able to soothe him. We tried everything to calm him down, but nothing worked.

Paul and I felt that those meltdowns from Kevin were our fault because we had done too much that day or had pushed him past his point of tolerating running around town. He wanted to be back in his own home where things were quiet and peaceful where he could relax. Now to us, we were only thinking about getting a quick bite to eat, so I didn't have to cook at home. It wasn't ever any fancy restaurant, just fast food or family dining types, but Kevin sure knew when to throw a fit; it was usually always about the time the food arrived. We would either get our food to go, or one of us would take him outside to calm down while the other would eat and then we would switch, which wasn't any fun at all.

During those times I would think to myself, "I should have just gone home and made a home-cooked meal. It probably would have been healthier for us all, and cheaper too." With keeping up with a baby and work, however, Paul and I were often just too exhausted to do that on a regular basis. In the midst of that exhaustion, and looking back now, I wonder if there were early warning signs of his struggles to come that were then slowly starting to appear.

On Kevin's first birthday, we had family and friends to our house for a celebration. I remember buying Kevin an adorable shirt which cost $25.00. That was a lot to spend on a shirt for a growing baby, but it was so cute, I couldn't resist buying it. I wanted him to look good in his pictures, and he did look great until he ate the chocolate birthday cake I had baked him! The cake was all over him and his new shirt. I never could get those chocolate stains out, but now, the memory just makes me smile.

It was getting late, and everyone decided to go out for dinner. I was so proud of my little boy and was bragging on him in a playful way saying that maybe someday he would be on TV. One of our friends commented that TV producers usually like giggly kids and those with a lot of expression. The comment stung, even though I knew it wasn't meant to be hurtful and was probably said without our friend realizing how her words sounded. I knew right away, however, that Kevin wasn't any of those things. Despite that, she was exactly right in describing Kevin's demeanor. He wasn't a giggly baby; he was more of a straight-faced, intense and serious baby. She was the first person to notice that something was a little different. Not bad, just different. I look back on that day as the first time I noticed that something was "not normal."

I read the parent magazines looking to pick up new ideas and ways to take care of my baby. I asked his Pediatrician about his development and if he was doing alright. Kevin's doctor always said he was doing well, and that everything was normal and on schedule for being born so early. Being a first-time parent, one wonders if something you see or hear your child do is normal behavior or not. Granted, all children are individual and different, but once in a while, something seemed to be amiss, in a way neither Paul nor I could exactly put our finger on.

There were times when he would cry for such a long time that it seemed abnormal. We always heard it was best to leave a baby to cry, and eventually they would stop on their own. Don't enter their room to console them because it would tell the child that if they cried long enough, someone would come to their rescue. Kevin didn't respond well to that idea. We tried it, but he would cry for hours. This seemed far beyond a normal situation of letting a baby cry themselves to sleep. He wasn't able to ever calm down. This was one of the early clues that something was very different with Kevin.

There was another time that we recognized something was disturbing was when Kevin was around three years old. Paul and I were going to the movies, and our son's Grandma Neubauer was going to watch him at our house that evening. Kevin got so upset that we were leaving and he threw a huge fit. He started banging his head on the floor and crying uncontrollably. He wasn't able to gain control over his emotions and cried for hours. We held him tight and rocked him and told him everything was going to be o.k., and that we weren't going anywhere. We tried to distract him and make him happy, but there didn't seem to be anything we could do to calm him down. Needless to say, we didn't go to the movies that night and were filled with a sort of dread at this intense behavior. It was frightening to see and was beyond what perhaps a more normal tantrum might look like.

Kevin also did this thing we would call "Doo Doo" mode. Whenever he started saying "Doo Doo, Doo Doo, Doo Doo," we knew we couldn't get through to him. It's as though he were in a trance, lost in his own little world. His speech was delayed a little bit, and later on, we found that his lingual frenulum (attached skin under his tongue) needed to be surgically clipped back. That was part of the reason it was initially so hard to understand what he was saying.

We noticed from an early age that he couldn't let go of a thought or feeling. He overreacted to little situations. Something as simple as asking him to put on his shoes or get dressed. If he didn't want to do it, he threw a fit. I know most children at some point or another can be prone to a melt down when they just aren't in the mood to do what is asked of them, but this was to such a constantly extreme level. He wasn't able to control his emotions and would cry uncontrollably, or huff and puff with a very angry look on his face. He wasn't even six years old, yet he showed *so* much anger and frustration. Much more frustration than any child should feel and experience at that age. He was very persistent, and if he got it in his head that he didn't want to do something, that was it. He was going to rebel. We always thought that his reactions didn't seem to fit whatever had just happened. Everything was an overreaction, but that was how he felt. He just wasn't able to cope.

I remember when Kevin was around three years old, and we took a Mommy and Me class together. Kevin met a cute little-redheaded girl named Sarah, and he was instantly attracted to her. Every time we went to class, he instantly gravitated toward her. She was his friend. We all sat in a circle and sang songs like "No Monkeys Jumping on the Bed," and we did some fun craft projects. When Christmas time came, the class held a Christmas party, and Santa Clause was there. It was the first time that Kevin got to sit on Santa Clause's lap. It was a fun group and was our special time together, and he seemed pleasant and content when we were there.

We weren't sure why Kevin reacted in ways that didn't make a lot of sense to us. We weren't sure what to even call them. We asked different doctors, counselors, psychologists, and psychiatrists, and they didn't have an explanation either.

We were still living in Ontario, California when Kevin was around four or five years old. For Christmas that year, Paul and I bought him a swing set that we had found together at the Sears Clearance Center near our house. It was a very large, blue swing set, and the price was so good that we bought it right away. We brought it home and hid it in the garage and were so excited to give it to him and see his reaction to it on Christmas day! We thought it was a great present and assumed that he'd be so excited when he saw it that he would run over to it and start playing on it right away. Boy, were we wrong. It's kind of like when kids like playing with the box more than the great present. He could care less about the new swing set. He tried it for about a minute and wasn't interested anymore.

There were a lot of times where Kevin didn't show much excitement at all. As a parent, you want to expose your child to as many new things as possible in the world and teach them about many subjects so they can decide what they like and don't like. It's good for them to make their own decisions. We enjoyed presenting different games, sports, nature walks and toys so Kevin could decide for himself. That's part of the fun of being a parent also; sharing with your child and connecting. Some days, however, it seemed as if we weren't connecting with him at all.

Kevin was slow in learning how to ride a bicycle, even with the training wheels. He just peddled slowly. That was his pace...slow. I remember going on walks with him as he rode his bicycle and I kept up with him when I was just walking. He was very content going at his own pace and didn't want to speed things up. We tried to get him to go faster, but he wouldn't have anything to do with it. He peddled slowly and evenly without a care in the world. He was having fun – but in his own way.

Kevin may have peddled slowly on a bicycle, but he was going fast on my brother Larry's go-kart one day when we were visiting him in Newberry Springs. Kevin was around six or seven years old when this happened. My brother lived on an acre of land with a man-made lake in the center. He had a dock for fishing, a goat, chickens, a mini potbelly pig, two cats, and a dog. Kevin was riding this go-cart around the lake and was driving it by himself when the throttle became stuck wide open, and since it was stuck on full speed (about 30mph) around the lake, he couldn't stop it. He was getting really scared, and Paul and Larry were yelling for Kevin to go towards the water. They figured that water would be the softest landing. Well, Kevin didn't know how to swim yet, and going into the water was the last choice on his mind. Paul and Larry tried to stop the go-cart, but it was very difficult. They figured if he drove towards the fence and hit it, he could get pretty banged up. How about running into Daddy? Maybe that would be the best option. Water, fence or Daddy? What did Kevin choose? Daddy, of course. Kevin steered towards Paul coming head on, at full speed. Paul grabbed the go-kart and held onto it slowing it down a little, just enough for it to go up over his back, leaving chain and tire tread marks across him. Larry came and shut off the go-kart. It was painful for Paul, but it all ended well since Kevin didn't get hurt in the whole ordeal. I was inside cleaning Larry's house, and I'm sure glad I didn't see any of it, or I would have been screaming my head off and running after the go-cart like a crazy mom. That was one adventure that this mom didn't need to witness!

Another struggle Kevin had was that he couldn't follow three directions at a time. For example, go put your shoes on and brush your teeth, then come into the kitchen when you are finished. I remember at one of his doctor's appointments, the doctor asked if Kevin could follow in sequential order three directions that were given to him. I had to think very hard, but for the life of me I couldn't think of one time where Kevin was able to do that. He might do two of the things that were asked, but not all three, and most of the time was only able to follow through on one.

When one of his first teachers at the Montessori school wanted to get his attention, she would say to him "Look at my eyes," and she would be pointing at her eyes. Then she had his full attention, and he would listen to her. That was genius!

It wasn't important to Kevin to be able to do what you were asking of him. He got along in life by doing what he wanted to do in his own way. It was very trying at times to communicate with him and have him do what was asked. Professionals talk about setting boundaries and having consequences for various actions. It sounds simple, but it was difficult to execute a lot of the time. We tried many different behavioral management techniques to get Kevin to perform a simple task. His doctors even said that bribery was alright too, and we would develop different incentive games to try to inspire him to do what we wanted him to do, or to learn how to do a particular thing. He would earn either money or a trip to the coin shop, or something from the grocery store, or a new video game. We tried everything we could think of. We used sticker charts, golf tees on a pegboard, marbles, signs on his bedroom door, and notes in his lunchbox, all with incentives. He was a tough cookie to get some action out of. We knew something was wrong but wouldn't find out until much later.

There were other signs of Autism, but we hadn't identified them as such. Autism or Asperger's Syndrome or Autistic Spectrum Disorder were words we hadn't heard of until many years later. One psychologist described normal behavior as going from point "A" to point "B" to point "C," but with Kevin, "B" was missing. That's exactly what it felt like when we were trying to get through to him or describe his behavior to doctors or teachers. It wasn't easy to explain, and we didn't have a name for it either. It was like walking blind, trying to treat something that was nameless and had no shape - that feeling of walking through the unknown was sometimes terrifying, especially when it affected Kevin's ability to connect with others and make friends.

When he was around four or five years old, we went to Lake Havasu City to visit family. There is a nice beach area there with a playground. We were walking along the beach and around the playground area, and Kevin wanted to play on the play structure. We were encouraged, seeing him want to engage with other kids. He walked up to a child that was playing and asked him "Do you want to be my friend?" They looked at him funny and ran off, leaving Kevin standing all alone. It was an awkward moment. He didn't realize that what he was saying wasn't something you would say to any kid playing, that you had never seen before or played with before. Normally kids would just start playing together naturally, but that wasn't natural for Kevin.

We felt so bad for him and embarrassed at the same time. No child wants to feel rejected, and he didn't understand why the other kids didn't want to play with him. At the same time, we felt embarrassed as parents that we hadn't prepared for how to talk to him about rejection. I guess Paul and I were never good at dealing with it either, and it's hard to teach what you don't know yourself.

Other times he would walk up to a stranger and ask the same question, "Would you be my friend?" Kids close to his age would laugh at him. I remember having many conversations explaining why that wasn't an appropriate question, why he got laughed at, and how he could play with the other children without asking them if it was ok. It's hurtful when you see your child struggling to do the simplest thing – playing on a playground. We knew right then that what he was exhibiting wasn't normal behavior.

Kevin was between five and six years old when he was playing at one of our neighbor's houses who has five children in their family. He was well aware that he didn't have any brothers or sisters and was all alone at his house and he began saying to us, every so often, that he wished he had a brother or sister. We would tell him "Well maybe someday, but for now, you are the very best, and you are so very special to us." He kept talking about a brother or sister for about a year. Finally, one day when he was around six or seven years old, we decided to tell him that he did have a sister, but she died. She was his twin sister, her name was Heather, and she lived about two days. We explained to him how he and his sister were born so early, and that he was a twin and what that meant, and how most twins are born on the same day. We told him that they were extra special twins because she was born eleven days and seven hours before he was born, so they each had their own birthdays. He seemed alright at first when we told him about his sister, but a few days later he expressed to us that he was sort of upset with us because we had never told him about her. I think he was feeling sad for her, and he was feeling lonely too. We questioned ourselves for a long time about whether to tell him or not, and I guess we told him a little too early for his mind to process the information. A few years later he told us that he was sad about it and wished that we hadn't told him. He was sad and missed her, even though he had never met her. She was a part of him, and he was grieving her loss.

Later on, there were times when we would be standing in a grocery store line, for example, and someone would say to Kevin, "You are such a cute little boy. Do you have any brothers or sisters?" He would say "I had a sister, but she died." They never knew how to react, and most people don't expect to hear that answer coming from a young boy, so they felt really bad for asking in the first place. I appreciated that about Kevin, though, for his honest perception of the world, and for his childlike boldness to speak his mind in the way he did.

His Grandma Walker remembers when she, Kevin, and I were shopping in a shoe store in Lake Havasu City. I was trying on shoes for myself, and I wanted Kevin to find some shoes also. She said to Kevin "Why don't you let that nice lady help you try on some shoes?" and he said "I don't "ike" that nice lady." Grandma thought that was the cutest thing she had ever heard...I don't "ike" that nice lady. One never knows what kids will say.

He always kept us on our toes, as all children do. Kevin attended a Montessori school from preschool through the first couple months of first grade. After school, either Paul or I would pick him up and bring him to our mortgage office until it was time for us to go home, and we would try to keep him occupied while we did some work. There was an old copy machine at the office that Paul didn't want any longer, so he showed Kevin how to take it apart. He gave Kevin some wire cutters and screwdrivers and said he could do whatever he wanted with the parts. He cut wires, unscrewed panels and kept busy taking apart the copier for quite some time. That's one way to keep an inquisitive six-year-old occupied!

A couple of weeks later, Kevin was in the garage with Paul, who was working on the air conditioning / heater igniter assembly. Paul had the side of the blower assembly open, and he wasn't paying attention to what Kevin was doing, who was happily occupied with Paul's wire cutters. Kevin proceeded to cut ALL of the control wires in the air conditioner! Did I mention it was summer in California? Kevin just did what he did earlier at the office. Paul couldn't get upset; in fact, he thought it was really funny! I initially thought we would need a repairman to come out to the house and rewire the air conditioner, but thankfully Paul is so talented, and he was able to rewire it himself. It wasn't easy, but he figured it out. I wouldn't necessarily blame that whole event on Autism, I just chocked it up to Kevin being a boy and "helping" his dad.

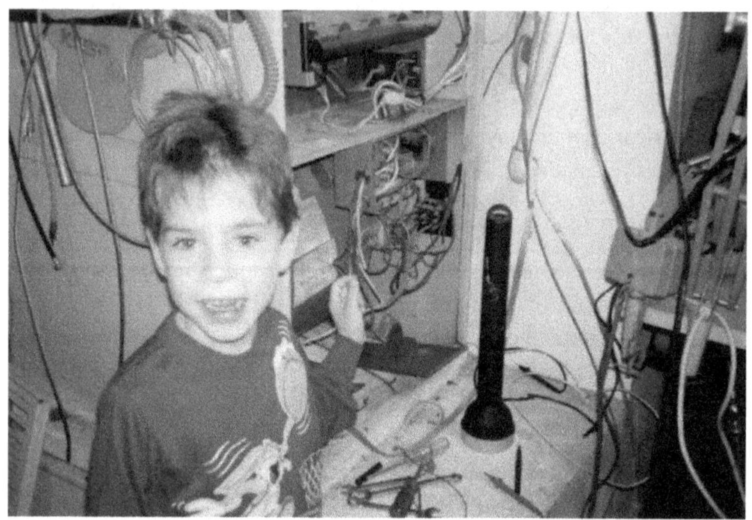

Kevin cut the air conditioner wires.
(How could you be mad at that cute little face?)

Later on, Paul and I thought we could take a short trip to Las Vegas and have a little fun. It was a much-needed break for the two of us, a chance to reconnect a bit and be alone as a couple. We asked Kevin's grandparents to watch him for us, and Grandpa Jack had some fun prepared. Kevin was really into collecting rocks, and so his Grandpa Jack thought it would be a great idea to paint some rocks gold; then he hid them for Kevin to find, who of course was so excited for when he found them! Grandpa Jack told Kevin that he could give them to us when we got back from Las Vegas and that we could turn them in for a lot of money. Kevin was on board and couldn't wait to show us. Jack just laughed; I guess he knew he had put us in a sticky situation!

Kevin had a hard time making friends at school. I felt so bad for him, because when I was his age, I felt shy and uncomfortable trying to join in and play on the playground as well. I knew from experience that what he was going through was lonely and isolating, and it was easy to feel like an outcast. It should be so easy to join in and just start playing and talking with the other children, but they can be mean at times, and sometimes just not understand kids who might be different than them. When Kevin was in the first or second grade, he began experiencing headaches and would make these strange movements with his head. He would strain his neck upward like he was trying to catch a breath. Sometimes he would stretch out his arm in a strange manner, or he would shiver as though he were suddenly ice-cold and jerk his body. Looking back, I have to wonder if perhaps those ticks he exhibited were a form of stress from his difficult days at school. We weren't sure, but we did take him to a neurologist to find out. The doctor ran some basic tests, and he gave Kevin "Neurontin" for his headaches. It helped a lot, but the ticks persisted, and they never went away completely.

It's still hard to understand why the professionals we so often got help from with Kevin were not able to recognize for some time that he had was a spectrum disorder, and that so many of his struggles came from this. Maybe at the time, it was too early to really know for sure. Kevin was considered high functioning, and sometimes he appeared "normal," but things changed quickly as he grew older. Everything was getting more difficult for him and trying to cope with daily life was a struggle. In Kevin's mind, he knew how he felt, even if his perception was that something was worse than it truly was. His emotions were still his emotions, and they were as real and valid as anyone else's. He felt so bad and just wanted to feel happy and experience acceptance.

Despite his early struggles to make friends and connect with his peers, Kevin did have a few good friends throughout the years. First, there was Timmy and Michael who lived across the street in Ontario. They would come over to our house and play on the swing set with Kevin or play video games (mostly video games) and would take turns playing at one another's homes. I always enjoyed watching them run around and play together; I guess they were all young enough to know that being nice to each other was more fun than bullying someone.

Then there was Catherine, whom Kevin met around age six and a half when we moved to Laguna Niguel, California. They were inseparable from the very first day on the bus ride to school and home again. They had common interests like collecting rocks, swimming, riding bicycles and just playing whenever they could. In fact, Kevin learned to ride a bicycle without the training wheels because of her. Catherine's dad, along with Paul and I, went to a baseball field one day at a nearby school. Catherine's dad was convinced that Kevin would learn to ride his bike if it was in the soft dirt. He was right! It only took a few minutes, and Kevin was riding on his own. It was incredible to watch, not to mention seeing someone teach our son something like that, in a way that would reach Kevin in a way he needed. Kevin and Catherine always had a great time together. I think she was the love of his life for many years, and he kept all the special notes she wrote him for many years after moving away from that area.

LET'S TRY TO HAVE A SIBLING

We tried a couple more times to have another baby. So far, we had been lucky in "getting" pregnant, compared to other couples who try many times before achieving pregnancy and sometimes it never works for them.

Dr. Asch performed the GIFT procedure again for our second try, a couple of years after Kevin was born, and I got pregnant that time also; however, he said I had a biochemical miscarriage a couple of weeks later because my HCG levels didn't continue increasing. I barely knew I was pregnant; no morning sickness, no other symptoms; the pregnancy was over.

Then we tried an In Vitro Fertilization (IVF) procedure (third try) in the doctor's office instead of having surgery at the hospital, and I got pregnant again! We felt so fortunate to be pregnant again. Then around ten weeks along the heartbeat stopped. I know this because I had an ultrasound every week after they had found I was pregnant, so it was just routine to have my blood drawn and have the ultrasound done weekly. On week nine the baby was fine, then the next week things were different. I knew the ultrasound didn't look right. I even said something to the technician doing the ultrasound. He left the room and came back with a doctor to double check everything. The doctor confirmed that the heartbeat had stopped. We were shocked. It was such a sad moment when they confirmed what I had noticed...I didn't see the heart beating. I was really beginning to feel pregnant, and my stomach had already swelled a little bit; excitement was building more and more each day as I began to anticipate the changes in my body and look forward to giving birth.

There must have been something wrong with the embryo to not survive. The doctors say that when something like this happens, it's one way our bodies take care of an unhealthy situation. I'm so glad Paul was with me that day at the office visit. I cried and felt heartbroken knowing that the pregnancy was over. It was completely unexpected. It had been ten weeks; that's seventy days that Paul had given me my progesterone injection every morning to stay pregnant. I would have had only thirty more days of injections, but now that the baby's heartbeat had stopped the doctor told me to stop my progesterone injections and I was told I would most likely miscarry the fetus. The doctors weren't sure at what point the placenta takes over in a pregnancy and when the progesterone shots weren't necessary anymore. They didn't know if my hormone levels would just drop, and I would naturally miscarry or whether I would have to have a D&C to fully end the pregnancy.

A little more than a week went by, and I started to miscarry. Grief is interesting that way, how you can walk around not knowing it's there some days, and then something happens, like miscarrying again. After going through so much already, including losing our daughter Heather, the end of this pregnancy brought some of those feelings up to the surface again. The beautiful thing about grief is that no matter how painful it can be to live with, it's truly a reminder of how much love there has been, and still is, for the babies we have lost.

ELEMENTARY SCHOOL YEARS

Kevin was in the second grade, and the school thought it would be beneficial to refer him for an assessment because he appeared somewhat depressed to the school staff. In speaking with his teachers, we had mentioned it as well. It concerned us that for at least six months he continually made self-negative comments and had said things like "I just want to kill myself!" "I hate my life!" or "I wish I were dead!" He had few friends and lacked social skills, and his school ended up testing him for Special Education classes.

At the testing, his Behavioral Observation was that he seemed wary and reluctant. Throughout testing, he appeared quite anxious as to his performance and very upset at "having" to be tested. His body language appeared very rigid; facially – bored, angry and worried. Eye contact was limited, and he rarely smiled and displayed a flat affect. He also verbalized his displeasure with being there, many times. According to the Impressions/Summary from the Speech/Language Pathologist: *"Kevin shows age-appropriate skills in voice, fluency, oral motor, and articulation skills. Pragmatics (conversation) appear affected by Kevin's personality, being somewhat "withdrawn." Vocabulary skills appear to be age appropriate. Language fundamentals appear average except assigning words to a "class" from when asked to choose "which two words go together" from three or four examples. There was considerable confusion in Kevin's ability to listen to paragraphs and recall the details when questioned."*

This evaluation allowed the school to provide extra assistance for Kevin. They developed an Individualized Education Program (IEP) for him. Now the school could provide him with extra one on one help and adjust his assignments if he was falling behind. It was such a big help at the time. You could see him struggling and getting frustrated in school, and he was only in the second grade. I'm grateful that the school realized that something needed to be adjusted for him to succeed academically. This type of program allowed a child to thrive while at their level of learning, and also was able to reduce the amount of frustration the teacher might have been having with a particular student; it was helpful for them in knowing more clearly that certain students have different learning styles.

The summer after second grade we enrolled Kevin at The Sylvan Learning Center in Laguna Hills for their reading program. It was there that he became interested in the *Goosebumps* books. The school spurred his interest in reading, and he improved greatly. The Sylvan Learning Center kept their promise that they would raise his grade level by one or two grades after attending the school for five months. That's exactly what he did. It was expensive but well worth it. He gained a new self-confidence and a love for reading. He was hooked on the Goosebumps books, and he had to have ALL of them. That was fine with us! It kept him reading. He also attended the Kumon Math Center which helped him in his math skills. It wasn't as much fun, according to Kevin, because there was homework to do after class with Kumon. Sounds like a kid. Overall, I would still recommend both programs for learning.

Kevin had problems in school not just academically, but socially as well. He had trouble making friends, and aside from the two friends in our neighborhood that he got along with, it was difficult for him to connect and get along with other children. Kids at school would tell him to shut up when Kevin only looked at them. They could oftentimes be cruel, perhaps out of fear that he was different than them and not knowing how to respond. Kevin felt unwanted and unwilling to go to school. Every morning was a hassle to even get him out of bed in the morning, and I tried many different things like bribery, tickling, pulling the covers off of him, turning on the lights in his bedroom, and threatening to pour water on him and just annoying him in general, just to get out of bed. Paul always thought he needed a bed like a toaster where the bed would eject him out of bed and onto his feet.

After school, I always asked him how his day went, and we would talk about it. Some days were ok, and other times he would say that he hated his life. He hated everything about it. That was coming from a nine-year-old boy. He would say things like, "I hate my life, I wish I were dead, I don't want to live, it's too hard for me, I feel like a dummy, I feel like something is missing in my brain, I'm stupid, the kids call me a dummy." It was heartbreaking for me to hear him talk this way; sometimes I would find notes in his bedroom and in his backpack of how he felt. He was really struggling. It was so sad to hear him talk this way, to read these things, knowing he was suffering so much inside, especially when he would use the words, "I wish I were never born." It struck us so deep down in our hearts because we knew how much we always wanted him and our love ran so deep for him and what we went through to give birth to him. He was such a blessing to us, and we were so grateful to have him in our lives. For him to wish he was never born was such a sad and strong feeling for a young boy to be feeling. In the beginning, I started saving some of his notes, but I also remember throwing many of them away, thinking that this was just a phase he was going through. Unfortunately, there were many more notes in the years to follow.

PART THREE: A LIFE OF UPS AND DOWNS

DECEPTION

We were living in Laguna Niguel, California. It was so beautiful there; just two miles from the beach the way the crow flies, and about a seven-mile drive. It was close enough to appreciate the fresh ocean air with cool, foggy mornings and beautiful days. To this day, that's been our very favorite place to live. It was a long drive for Paul to make to Pasadena, but he did it every day for over three years.

Kevin turned seven in February of 1995, and though we were having our challenges at school, it was nothing like what was about to turn our lives upside down. In May of that same year, the Orange County Register broke the news of a scandal, stating that internationally renowned fertility specialists Dr. Ricardo Asch and Dr. Jose Balmaceda had taken patients eggs for research without the consent of the patient. Eggs were fertilized and implanted in a second woman, and she gave birth. There were many more articles reporting different cases of stolen eggs and embryos. We didn't think this could be possible.

There was no way our doctors would do anything dishonest like that. We even wrote a letter of support to the doctors telling them how unbelievable this scandal sounded and expressed our feelings of disbelief and concern for them. We believed there was *no possible way* they could have done what they were being accused of doing. We thanked them for being so loving, caring, and professional in helping us to achieve pregnancy. We were so grateful to them and the woman who had donated her eggs to us.

Hundreds of more articles appeared on the web and in the newspaper over the next several months. We looked at the documents in the newspaper where they crossed out names of patients and donors, and we didn't see anything that matched us. That was a relief. I couldn't even imagine how horrible it would feel to find out that eggs were stolen from you. It was a violation and theft of unspeakable terms. Those women's bodies had been violated of something as special and personal as an egg that could produce life, and it was taken without consent. I felt devastated for the women who were affected. This news went on for over six months in the newspaper.

"The University of California, Irvine, was severing its ties with the prestigious Center for Reproductive Health amid allegations that doctors conducted unapproved medical experiments on patients." May 16, 1995, Orange County Register

Then one day we saw one of the medical logs in an article that looked like it might be the dates when I had my GIFT procedure, but thankfully, upon closer inspection we knew that it wasn't. We held our breath every time more information came out, hoping it wouldn't involve us.

Over the next several months, we listened to the news reports and were in total denial that we could ever be mixed up in the fertility scandal. It seemed like a couple of times a week; Paul would bring home another article he had found online. We felt so bad for the others who had their eggs and embryos stolen. It was just sickening and unimaginable.

In an article published in July 1995 in the Orange County Register, there were new cases found involving women at the clinic at AMI–Garden Grove Medical Center, where the doctors worked from 1986 until 1990 before moving to the UCI Center for Reproductive Health in Irvine. I felt my heart stop when I discovered that article, as that is where I was treated and got pregnant with the twins from donated eggs. Who were involved in these new cases found? It surely couldn't be me. There were always so many patients at the AMI–Garden Grove Medical Center doctor's office when I was there. The front office was always filled with patients waiting to either see a doctor, have blood drawn or have a procedure right in the office. What are the odds that this scandal would come knocking on our front door? We felt it was slim to none.

Not long after, we heard about FBI agents who raided the clinic in Laguna Hills at the Saddleback Medical Center and copied computer files and took business records, embryo logs and containers of frozen embryos and all medical records for patients who started seeing the doctor before 1995. There was also an FBI raid on Dr. Asch's home in Newport Beach where they searched his belongings. There were rumors that embryos might have been destroyed. The devastating information was in the newspapers and all over the news reports on television. It became nerve-wracking to hear almost every day, knowing that we still had three frozen embryos there. We were so afraid we might lose all access to them and didn't want to lose our opportunity to try for the last time to build our family and have a little brother or sister for Kevin. Paul and I kept asking each other, "Would our embryos still be there for us to use? Were they destroyed in the FBI raid?" We simply didn't know and continued to wait.

Finally, I called the Saddleback Medical Center to inquire about our embryos and where they were. They said we would be able to use them if we decided to do so. Paul and I talked about it, and we made the decision to use our last embryos through an in-vitro procedure at the Laguna Hills office. It was August 8, 1995, and our very last try at getting pregnant. The procedures were expensive and were already blessed with a child, and we had spent a lot of money on the previous three procedures. This time would be our final attempt. We couldn't just let our embryos go unused, and we didn't know what the future would hold with the fertility scandal that was now in the news almost every day. Maybe our embryos would end up getting lost. We had to try one last time.

This was our fourth attempt to grow our family. We had three frozen embryos leftover from the previous attempt to use for a future try. We didn't want to lose the opportunity to use our embryos, as the FBI could have confiscated them, and we might never have access to them again; they could also get lost somewhere with all the confusion and deception going on. We thought we'd better act fast and proceed with the transfer before our last chance was gone; Paul and I knew we had to try. This particular donor wasn't the same as Kevin's donor, but nonetheless, she was so very special and important to be willing to donate her eggs to someone who needed them. When I went in for the IVF procedure, the nurses described the donor's appearance. She was a little taller than me and had darker hair, but that was o.k. We wanted to have a sibling for Kevin.

The doctor transferred three frozen embryos through in-vitro fertilization in the doctor's exam room that day. We crossed our fingers and hoped for the best. This time after the procedure, the first two weeks felt a little different to me. I wasn't sure what it was and tried to keep positive that everything would turn out alright, but I was feeling some doubt.

Maybe those were my instincts kicking in.

Maybe I already knew the answer.

Two weeks after the transfer, I returned to the doctor's office for my pregnancy blood test. I was feeling a little apprehensive that day, and unfortunately my instincts were correct, and I wasn't pregnant. It was the only time where I didn't achieve pregnancy out of four tries. It was very disappointing, but at the same time, I was at peace knowing we at least tried to get pregnant with everything that was going on with the doctor's other facility. That certainly could have caused extra stress at the time, looking back, and I wonder if that was a contributing factor as to why the pregnancy didn't happen.

A short time after finding out that I wasn't pregnant, I went to my regular family physician, and they tested my thyroid levels as I had routinely done. The doctor found that my Thyroid levels were out of balance, which for me meant that I wasn't going to get pregnant and was most likely the reason why I didn't get pregnant during our last attempt. When I found out the levels were "off," it felt like we just threw away our embryos. I wished I had tested my thyroid levels before the procedure, and it was also a big "oops" on the doctors. They should have routinely checked them as standard protocol before doing a procedure on me. There are so many factors that go into being able to get pregnant normally, and when you have a medical procedure to assist, it's even more crucial.

Meanwhile, the fertility scandal with the doctors was growing. There were new articles all the time:

> *"November 4, 1995, the Orange County Register reported that at least sixty women were unknowingly involved in illicit egg or embryo transfers by the doctors. It was double the number of patients that the university officials previously acknowledged."*

I just kept telling myself; *This couldn't be true. The doctors couldn't possibly have done what they are being accused of doing.*

NEWSPAPER CALLED

I'll never forget the evening that I received a phone call from The Orange County Register. It was right after dinner. I was standing in the kitchen, and this man on the other end of the line identified himself and then asked if I was Joyce Tejan and if I was a patient of Dr. Ricardo Asch at the AMI–Garden Grove Medical Center in 1987. The conversation was making me feel very uncomfortable. Why would a newspaper reporter be calling me and how would he know this information about me? How did he get my phone number? What was going on? I said yes, he was speaking to Joyce. This reporter proceeded to tell me that he had information about the GIFT procedure I had on August 24, 1987. He even knew the correct date of when it took place. He asked if I had seen the news articles in the newspaper and on television about the scandal the doctors were involved in. I said, "Yes, I have seen some of it." I told him however that I didn't think it was true, and that there was no way the doctors could have done the things they were being accused of doing.

Then he said that he had information that showed that the eggs I received that day were from a donor who didn't intend on donating eggs to anyone. The doctors stole them from her. I was in shock. I didn't believe him, and I felt as though I had just been kicked in the stomach.

The man asked if he could meet with Paul and I and discuss what information he had, and to show us the documents where it showed me as the recipient of the eggs. He also told me that the donor lived about two miles from our house. That was so incredible, to hear and very uncomfortable at the same time. It couldn't really be happening, could it?

We agreed to meet the next evening. I hung up the phone and told Paul what this reporter had said on the phone. We were both in disbelief and very upset after his phone call. We talked about the conversation in depth and reviewed the newspaper articles we had saved. It was hard to sleep that night. Paul and I told each other that we would just have to wait and see what documentation the reporter was bringing for us to look at. We decided to tape record the conversation with him, because we wanted to be able to remember every word he said and have documentation should we need it. This reporter was coming over to our house to talk with us, and Kevin, our son, would be in the house as well. We knew very well that Kevin wouldn't stay in the other room and watch TV; he would want to be right out in the middle of everyone to hear what was going on. We needed to send him to his friend's house for an hour or so while we talked in private, and we were also nervous that this newspaper reporter might be there to take photos of Kevin or do something deceitful. I think my brain was on overload, and I desperately needed to just calm down so we could have a clear conversation with this man and listen to what he had to say.

The doorbell rang, and Paul and I tried to appear calm as we answered the door. The reporters name was David Parrish. He was a very nice man who seemed sympathetic to what we were going through, and as we sat down to talk, he showed us the papers he had with my name on them, as well as the date of the egg transfer and how many eggs I received and the result of the procedure. It was all there in black and white. It matched me as far as the dates and number of eggs and the result. We described to the reporter our side of the story and what we knew about the donor and how my GIFT procedure came about, and how we knew about two weeks in advance that it might be happening on August 24, 1987. He said the woman's eggs whom I received had a laparoscopy to find out why she couldn't carry a pregnancy to full term. It was an exploratory procedure as far as she had been concerned. That's what we knew also; we thought she had the laparoscopy to see why she couldn't get pregnant. But what we didn't know was that she did not consent for her eggs to be donated to anyone. This is where Dr. Asch crossed the line. The events that led up to that day make it so clear now. Dr. Asch had to have known that this would be the woman whose eggs would be implanted into me.

All the pieces of the puzzle from the fertility scandal and the documents the news reporter brought that evening was, unfortunately, making too much sense. We were in utter shock that something like this could happen, and full of disappointment in the doctors we had grown to respect and trust. We were in immediate fear of losing our child, who was the love of our life and our entire world. After the reporter left our house, we went to pick up Kevin who was at the neighbor's house, and just hugged him tightly hoping and praying nothing would ever take him from us.

That night changed our lives forever; from that point on, life would never be the same. The reporter said that the donor mom didn't have any intentions of interfering in taking Kevin away from us, but what if she changed her mind later on? Anything could happen. Paul and I were extremely nervous and were wracked with anxiety. I felt this shaking feeling every time I thought of all that had happened and was sick to my stomach. It was a nightmare, a total living nightmare that could not be escaped by waking up.

The reporter wrote a very nice article called "Two women are linked by child one has never seen." (November 11, 1995, Orange County Register) Paul and I were so afraid that the donor mother could someday try and take Kevin away from us. What if she wanted visitation rights? Maybe she would drag us through the courts and take him away from us. We had our child that was biologically half hers, and she didn't have anything, except a nightmare of her own. With all of this going on, we also had Kevin's mental health struggles and difficulties in school to deal with, and the thought of putting him through any added stress felt overwhelming in a way I still don't have words for.

One piece of information we learned from the article published was that the woman whose eggs were stolen and given to us had never had a baby herself, and recently had a hysterectomy. Through the newspaper article, we also learned that she and her husband had adopted several children, including a set of twins. She said, *"Being the mother of adopted children, she understands the nagging fear of having another person suddenly show up claiming parental rights." "I would never do that,"* she said. *"I understand whoever this woman is, she never wants to hear from me."*

Years earlier we had written a thank-you letter to the donor mom after the GIFT procedure and gave it to the fertility clinic workers to deliver it. That message we now know was never given to her because she never consented to donate her eggs. They couldn't ever give her our letter of appreciation because she had no idea the doctors were harvesting eggs from her, let alone the fact that they had been given to a stranger.

Even amidst these awful events, we wanted her to know, whoever she was, that we were so grateful to her for donating her eggs to us and that we were sorry for the circumstance in which her body was violated. We would never have wanted eggs from someone who never intended to give them. The reporter delivered that letter to her.

A few weeks later, after meeting with the Orange County Newspaper reporter, we received a call from a producer of ABC News, Primetime Live with Diane Sawyer. She wanted background information for the Primetime Live show about our relationship in the fertility scandal. They wanted to do a story about what happened, but we said we didn't want to talk to them. We were too afraid, fearing it would lead to losing Kevin forever. It was too risky. We benefited from the GIFT procedure, and this other woman did not. We were the ones who would be on the losing end of this nightmare of a situation now.

The week of December 11, 1995, we were contacted again by ABC News from the Los Angeles area, and they wanted to do a "meet and greet," just to talk with us. That was scary also, but for some reason, we said yes to the reporter coming over to our house. We made an early morning appointment, and she said she would bring some breakfast, which she did. She brought bagels, and we talked for a short time. Kevin was a late sleeper, and we were pretty sure that he wouldn't wake up while she was there. If he did, that might give her some new juicy information that we felt she might be hoping to get. He didn't wake up, and we didn't tell her anything new that hadn't already been said. I presume she was looking for new details or some angle for her story. Well, we didn't give her anything; we were very guarded and nervous talking with her. I could tell she was disappointed with the meeting, even though she was very professional and polite.

Just when you think that everything that could happen had already happened...there's more. I received a phone call from the FBI. I didn't think it was real.

I remember scrambling to turn down the TV and to grab some paper to write on so I could take notes on what this person was saying. He started out the conversation by verifying information with me about my relationship with the AMI-Garden Grove Medical Center and UCI and some dates associated with the fertility scandal. It sounded plausible that it really was the FBI calling, but I wanted to make sure. I wanted them to tell me how they obtained my information and asked what information they had. They said they had my file from UCI and they told me some of the details that would only be known if they were reading my medical file. It was enough information to believe that it was truly the FBI calling me. Not in my wildest dreams would I ever think the FBI would reach out to me, and even with all the newspaper articles and television reports in recent news, I never thought my information amounted to much. I guess it helped to build their case against the doctors and provided a timeline for the many families involved in this scandal. I answered all of their questions over the phone, and then I asked if I could have a copy of my file. He said yes, which I was surprised to hear. I didn't expect him to give me my medical file. Of course, they had copies of everything. A week later it came to me in the mail in an official envelope with the FBI address on it. It was just one more piece to the puzzle that confirmed what the first news reporter had told us.

After all of these events, it was becoming more uncomfortable living in Laguna Niguel. The reporter told us the evening we met that the donor mom lived about two miles away from us in Laguna Hills. We could have easily crossed paths. From that night forward, every time I went to the grocery store or anywhere actually, I would look around to see if there was a mom with a couple of kids who looked similar to me and where I might see a resemblance of Kevin in her. The nurse had said that we looked like we could be sisters. I have always had the feeling that we did cross paths, but never knew it.

Karate at seven years old

Paul and Kevin in Laguna Niguel, California

Joyce and Kevin in Laguna Niguel, California

MOVING AWAY FROM THE SCANDAL

Paul had been driving from Laguna Niguel to Pasadena every day for the past three and a half years to work each day. It was at least an hour to hour and a half one-way, and he really needed to live closer to where he worked. We began looking for a house that was closer to his job and ended up moving to Brea, California in July 1997. This was a good move for several reasons. We wouldn't be so close to the donor mom, and I know that I would feel much more comfortable putting some miles between us. I was always on edge everywhere I went in town, and it just became so uncomfortable feeling like I had to look over my shoulder. Realistically, looking back on everything, she said that she didn't have any intentions of interfering with us, but I just felt so insecure about the thought that she might change her mind and Paul and I could lose Kevin. That thought was just too unbearable. After moving to Brea, I did feel more secure living farther away from Laguna Hills California.

CHALLENGES FOR KEVIN

Kevin started fourth grade in Brea, and school was better for him in ways. He liked his teacher, Miss Riffel; she was his favorite. His grades improved and he was still enjoying reading the Goosebumps books. He received several reading awards and Student of the Month, and his math skills improved greatly also. His confidence level was increasing. Things were looking up. Then, one day he brought home a letter from his teacher that said:

> *"Today Kevin was in line at the end of recess, and he tried to kiss Stephanie. We talked about this, and he said he wasn't "really" going to do it. However, we discussed the fact that it was not appropriate behavior for a fourth grader and he apologized to Stephanie. I did send him to a thirty-minute detention after lunch as a consequence for his actions. I just wanted to make you aware. I think he learned his lesson." -Miss Riffel*

I smile every time I think about this. I think Miss Riffel handled the situation just perfectly – a talk explaining what's appropriate and what's not, then having him apologize for his error, and a consequence afterward.

He was tested again in the fourth grade for his IEP assessment at his new school. The assessment revealed a significant discrepancy between cognitive ability and achievement in reading and written language, stating that processing disorders were noted in his auditory and visual processing. We read that he needed teacher reinforcement to begin tasks and to work independently, and that he returns homework most of the time.

Then in the fifth grade, his teacher said his reading skills were strong, and he tested one-half year above grade level. His spelling skills were weak, but writing samples were stronger. Math skills were one and one-half years above grade level.

That was very nice to hear. We hoped that school would get better for Kevin, and that he would be able to start making more friends.

One day the school announced, "no more yo-yos" were allowed because a boy was doing "Around the World," and hit himself in the head, so the ambulance was called out to the campus. A couple of days after this school event, Kevin wrote me a note:

> *"I tried to hit myself with my yo-yo in the head. Now I don't feel good, and my head hurts bad! Please don't remind me about this or talk to me about this or tell dad. I feel dizzy now!"*

Well, of course, I was going to have a talk with him. He was hurting. I left him alone for a while, and later I said to Kevin, "You did that just because another boy at school did it, right?" Kevin got this silly little grin on his face. He knew that I knew what and why he did this. It's amazing what experiments a ten-and-a-half-year-old boy will do out of curiosity.

Middle school can be a difficult time for a lot of kids. There appears to be more bullying around age ten to twelve, and it's more hurtful. It's not that bullying starts around that age, I believe it begins many years earlier; however, during the middle school years their hormones are changing, and they want to be accepted by their peers more than ever. They are becoming young adults, and everything is exaggerated and more important at this time. Kevin's dad also had troubles in school with bullying around the same age. Things became very uncomfortable. For that reason, we wanted to enroll Kevin in an environment that we thought would be a better transition for him. He had a couple of good school years in fourth and fifth grade, and we wanted to keep that trend going.

We enrolled him at Christ Lutheran Church and School in Brea for sixth grade. The staff was great, and we were very hopeful that Kevin would excel there. Unfortunately, sixth grade turned out to be very difficult. His attendance at school was worse than usual, and his grades weren't any better. The school tried to be accommodating to his needs, but he was too much to handle, and we withdrew him in the spring of the sixth grade.

I must have thought I was Superwoman and thought I could homeschool him and also work from home as a mortgage loan officer. I thought that if I wasn't able to get him out of bed and to school, then I could let him sleep in a little longer and start school at 10 am. It worked for a little while until he wouldn't perform for me, either. I heard of another private school, Carbon Canyon Christian School, where they rewarded the kids for good behavior by allowing them to take care of the horses and ride them. Kevin was interested in that and said he really wanted to go there, and we gave it a try. We had the same issues of getting him out of bed early to get to school on time, and his school work was not acceptable there either. We needed a new plan.

Seventh grade took us back to the public-school system. This time the school set an appointment for an Individualized Education Program (IEP) meeting right away at the beginning of the school year. They knew from his past school records that he needed some assistance.

Seventh grade was the time when students had to change classrooms for their different subjects. Kevin struggled in changing classes and getting there on time, and it was overwhelming for him. When they assessed him, they determined he didn't qualify for special education any longer because his grades had improved through the years nicely and was performing seventh-grade work at grade 6.5 to 8.3-grade level.

The assessment showed that he was still asking a lot of questions when trying to understand a concept. He also developed an anxious state when feeling too much pressure from school assignments and shut down and would complain so as to avoid school. He had a tremendous amount of difficulty organizing his school-related materials and school-related schedules, and also required much attention by school adults to keep him organized and on schedule. His seventh-grade teacher said "Kevin is a great kid. He does require extra assistance to complete ordinary school tasks." The school set a 504 plan to meet his needs and accommodate his performance in the classroom. It appeared his academic work had caught up nicely.

Kevin had encountered so many challenges in life so far, and things weren't getting much easier. There was always something occurring whether it be medical, social, educational, physical or mental in his life. We were acutely aware of his struggles, and it became a normal way of life for us to deal with it on a daily basis and do whatever we could to help him or find help for him. There were many times when Kevin would cry uncontrollably over a homework assignment, and this state of mind would continue on for a couple of hours. Sometimes he would cry himself to sleep. Other times he would lash out by hitting Paul or me or a door or wall.

It didn't take very much for Kevin to go into a rage. It could be something as simple as asking him to pick up his clothes off the floor or change into his Taekwondo uniform for class. It always boiled down to, well, anything he didn't want to do in the moment. He would act out in a fit. He had reacted that way for so long; it was how he got what he wanted. We tried setting boundaries and consequences for his actions, as well as coming up with incentive programs so he could feel the sense of accomplishment and be rewarded. It seemed like nothing worked well for very long until we had to come up with something else to get him to do what was asked of him.

There was this one day, it was after school, and Kevin wanted something. I think he wanted to play a video game, but he hadn't finished his homework yet, so I said "no." He got so angry that I wouldn't let him play his game, that he pushed me down on his bed and pinned me down and held down my hands. It was very scary. He was yelling in my face to give him the controller for the game. He was so strong that I couldn't get up off the bed. Paul was at work, and I didn't know how to get myself out of that situation. I decided to bite Kevin's arm, and it was just enough of a distraction to shock him, not believing that I would do something like that, and it made him let up on me enough that I got away from him. I remember him telling me later that he was really surprised that I bit him, that it really shocked him. I'm not sure if he ever understood how frightened I was, he just responded out of the tunnel vision and emotion he operated in; it was hard for him to ever take a breath first and think rationally.

We had already taken him to a couple of psychologists and behavioral counselors, and he had been through several school evaluations by this time in his short lifetime, but we decided to seek help from a Psychiatrist when he was ten and a half years old. We didn't want to medicate him, so the doctor evaluated Kevin for six months before we decided that we weren't getting anywhere, and maybe we needed to start him on psychiatric medicine.

It was February 9, 1999, when we made this very difficult decision, and it seemed like the best decision at that time. We felt we had exhausted everything else searching for ways to help Kevin feel better about himself and to experience the joy in life. Looking back on things now, we wish we never would have started him on medication; on the other hand, at the time we didn't see how Kevin could have survived mentally without it. Our decision tore our hearts apart. The doctor tried many different medications for his depression, OCD and anger outbursts, as well as chronic headaches. Once in a while, he would feel some relief, and we thought the doctor landed on the right cocktail of medicine for him. Then he would begin to have problems again so that the doctor would adjust the medicine or change Kevin to a different one.

During one of the adverse times, his anger outbursts became so extreme. He was yelling at both of us and was picking up things in his room and throwing them at us. We decided to restrain him on the floor. Paul held him on his stomach and sat on his back area holding his arms, and I held his legs down as Kevin whipped his head from side to side screaming at us. This went on for a good ten minutes or longer until finally, Kevin calmed down. I think his outburst might have been caused by the medication he was on. The doctor adjusted it the next day. Some medicine would make him so lethargic that he would want to sleep all the time or was so drowsy that he didn't care about his video games or anything. He didn't want to do anything - play games or do homework. That was equally as bad.

The Psychiatrist was very careful and conscientious about caring for him. He seemed conservative when changing Kevin's medicine and dosages. He was really trying to help our son, but it can be very difficult to treat mental health and behavioral health problems, especially in children. Each person is very different and reacts differently to various treatments. I don't blame the doctor for the outcome; I just wished Kevin felt more relief and was able to get better.

He also had environmental allergies and multiple ear infections and had tubes put in his ears twice to alleviate hearing problems. He has been through so much in his young life, and we were hoping at that time, that everything that needed to be done was done and Kevin would have smoother sailing going forward.

LOVE IN THE SHADOWS
SECOND COMMUNICATION

It was June 28, 1999, and I received a phone call from the Orange County Register again. It had been four years since the news broke about the stolen eggs and the fertility scandal accusing the doctors of mishandling many aspects at their medical offices. They wanted to do a follow-up story to find out how our lives had changed over the past four years and to ask how everything was going. We arranged a time when both Paul and I could be there to speak with the reporter over the telephone. This time it didn't feel as scary. The reporter we spoke to said that she had been in contact with the donor mom and had some information about her and thought we could pass some information back to her if we wanted to. We were excited to talk with the reporter this time. It was still a call that came out of nowhere, but at least it wasn't as unfamiliar as the first phone call four years earlier which was a nightmare.

This woman holds a very special place in our hearts, and I'd like to give her a very special name when speaking about her in this writing. Of course, I don't know her real name, so in my head, I began to refer to the "donor mom" as Christina Marie, which is the name we would have given our daughter if we had been able to have another one.

The reporter, Susan Kelleher, interviewed Christina and found out some specifics about her nationality, her background and how she had been doing since the news broke four years ago. We were very excited to exchange information that night. Paul and I went into one of our bedrooms and locked the door. We didn't want Kevin walking in on the conversation and us having to shew him away. I had my pen and paper out ready to take notes. What we found out that night was wonderful! It was comforting and a little bit healing too.

Her Father's side was one-hundred percent Dutch, and her Mother's Father was German. Her Grandmother was English. That was amazing because Paul's Father was German and his Mother was English. It was then that Paul and I felt a connection to her. She had wondered what Kevin looked like, and if he possibly looked at all like her father who had passed away a short time ago. At that time, we were thinking about Kevin's eyes and his eyebrows. Kevin's eyes were larger than Pauls' were and shaped differently, too. His eyebrows were bushy, and he had long eyelashes. They weren't mine nor were they Paul's. Maybe the bushy eyebrows came from his Dutch side.

We found out that it was a major shock when Christina first heard about the scandal, and we were told that she went into a deep depression. Questions plagued her, and thoughts like *"is love really a possession?"* swirled through her mind. I can imagine her saying to herself that her eggs were stolen from her body and that those eggs belonged to her. The result of those eggs was two living and breathing babies, Kevin and Heather; therefore, those babies were her possession. I don't know if this is what she was thinking, but if it was, I would have felt the same way too.

The love a mother has for her child is so strong and beautiful. It's much stronger than the feeling of possession. That feeling of love for Kevin was putting him first and doing what was best for him at that time. Just because you love someone, it doesn't mean you possess or own that someone. Christina could love the fact that Kevin was here, living and breathing and be happy for that fact, but he wasn't a possession to either Paul and I or Christina Marie. Kevin was his own person, being raised to be the best person he can be to himself. He was an individual being and didn't actually "belong" to anyone. I hope I'm doing justice in interpreting what I believe she meant when she said she thought about "whether or not love is really a possession."

She said she was in denial for a while, just like we were in the beginning. What snapped her out of her depression were her adopted twins and daughter. They needed her, and she wanted to be there for them.

She said she would meet him in Heaven many years from now. She talked about it many times and was asked if she was glad that it happened, and she said she was glad. She was glad because he was here, rather than *not* here, and looked at it as a gift - she understands her adoptive children better. She said she would love to see a picture of him and meet him someday, but she wouldn't want to meet as his "mommy's friend." It would be a lie to pretend to be someone she was not. She felt a lot of love for him and wanted to do the right thing. She had an ache in her heart and wanted to look at him and hold him. It was mystical that he was here, but he was here for a reason. We knew that after all he had gone through to get here.

According to the interview, she had no animosity towards UCI Medical Center. After all, it was the doctors making their ill decisions to do what they did to her. The medical center has a pet imaging center in which she currently enjoys donating to since she loves animals and had a lot of them while growing up. She said she had chinchillas, snakes, rabbits, and raised birds.

Her father and uncle were professional musicians. Her father played the trumpet in a big band, and her uncle played and taught in Buena Park. She taught elementary school for fifteen years, and her brother taught school also. He was a semi-pro tennis player at the state championship. She had trouble making friends, and she wasn't part of the "in" crowd either. She was well educated and had her BA and post-graduate degree.

She also said that she would be willing to give him anything he needed if Kevin got sick – a kidney or bone marrow transplant. Whatever he needed. If we needed to contact her, we could reach out to Larry Feldman who was her attorney, and he could pass information to her. What a wonderful and loving woman and mother she truly was. It felt so good to hear all of this through the reporter.

Kevin was now eleven years old, and we did want her to meet him some day after the difficult teenage years were over. During that time, though, we needed to make sure he had the emotional stability necessary to function and keep up with his studies. We passed along information to Christina about Kevin and what was new with him in school and his hobbies, how he played the piano and loved to read, and collected Beanie Babies, rocks, and coins. He was in Taekwondo and was three belts away from his black belt. He also loved doing magic tricks. He would practice for hours in front of his mirrored closet doors perfecting a magic trick. The sponge balls were his favorite at the time.

We didn't want to tell her of the struggles we were beginning to experience with him. There had been only a couple of serious outbursts, and his psychiatrist wasn't sure if they were hormonal (pre-pubescent) and it might end. We were hoping Kevin would grow out of them and life would be better for him. It didn't seem appropriate to spoil all the good news at the time.

The reporter wrote a beautiful article called Love in the Shadows, and it came out on July 4, 1999, in the Orange County Register. I wrote Christina a letter that she definitely should have received this second time. It was a thank you letter for all that she has done for our family. I also put together a photo album with about thirty pictures of when Kevin was a baby up to his current age of eleven, and I told her what his first name was. I drove to the Orange County Register to deliver the letter and photo album to one of the reporters who was working this story. I sure hope that Christina Marie received those pictures. We have wondered all these years if they were actually delivered to her. We were excited to share with her what we could at that time.

It's been very nice to look back on the article years later because there are details that I had forgotten. When reading it again, the words and feelings of that day come flooding back.

OBSESSIVE STAGES IN LIFE

Kevin would go through many different obsessive behaviors. They weren't as pronounced as some people's OCD habits you've probably heard about, but his were noticeable. Somehow, he would move from one obsessive behavior to another all on his own. One of the earliest habits was him turning his bedroom light switch on and off a bunch of times, and he had to tap on our car a few times. He also smelled his fingers a bunch of times and would jerk his neck upwards. We thought it was better to not make a big deal out of the different oddities he had. We figured that if we didn't draw too much attention to the behavior, he would eventually stop one obsessive behavior and pick up on another one. Which is what he did.

Many little boys like to play in the dirt and collect rocks. Kevin was no different. He would bring home special rocks every day. Some were very nice, and many were just ordinary, but he saw something special in all of them regardless. He and his friend Catherine would look intently for beautiful rocks on their walk home from the bus stop. They always came up with something they were in awe of, and they were always happy over whatever new special rock they had found together.

One day Kevin discovered the rock shop at the mall, which to him was better than finding a candy store. Whenever we would go to any mall, he would be looking for shops with rocks, and he found them. There was a wilderness store that he loved, and his dad and I dreaded taking him there if we were in a hurry, because we knew it would take at least an hour to get Kevin out of the store. We also knew it would cost us a few dollars. He was very selective choosing his purchases, and it always took a long time to decide. He would look at expensive rocks and then look at our faces, and he could always tell when we weren't going to buy certain rocks. I think he was trying to figure us out and wear us down at the same time finding out which rock we would be willing to buy for him. He did a pretty good job at that. All in all, his rock collection was very nice.

Then, around seven years old, he became interested in collecting coins. I'm not sure how it started, but I remember one day he absolutely had to go to this particular coin shop near our house. He was determined to buy a coin that day. We walked into the coin shop, and he became fixated on the foreign coins first. He would stare at them in the store for what felt like hours, and the salesperson told him he could choose about ten coins for just a couple of dollars. He really got excited then! Ten coins in Kevin's hand was a whole handful. He bought a variety of foreign coins that day, and that was the beginning of his collection. Then we taught him to look at the change he received when purchasing something, to see if there might be an "all silver" dime, or an "all silver" quarter, or maybe a "feather back" penny that he could add to his coin collection. We would save our silver coins and old pennies for him too. Then he would get coins for his birthday, and his collection began to grow. He also accumulated coins by joining coin clubs online. Periodically they held contests, and the prize would be a special coin. Kevin would have to either answer the quiz question or write an essay on something. Many times, he did win. He was very lucky and was always winning something or trading coins with other coin collectors. It was social as well as educational.

Kevin had his favorite television shows such as Power Rangers, Sonic the Hedgehog, and Mario Brothers. Pokémon came out, and the cards were his next big interest. His dad and I couldn't understand this. I guess it's like collecting baseball cards. Baseball cards can have a monetary value, but Pokémon cards were from a cartoon. Kevin researched the Pokémon cards and found the ones that were going to go up in value "for sure" he said. I couldn't believe it when we helped him purchase a fifty-dollar Pokémon card. Oh boy, did we feel taken that day! He thought it was the best thing he had ever bought, and he was on cloud nine. One day we heard that that card was worth a hundred dollars. "Wow!" we thought. Did we sell it for a profit? No. Kevin couldn't part with it. So much for making a profit on Pokémon cards. Oh well, he did have a nice collection that he was proud of, and that was more important to see that gleam in his eyes and that he was happy with the collection he had put together.

Eventually, the rocks, coins, and Pokémon cards took a back seat, and beanie babies took center stage. They were all the rage in the late nineties, and most of the elementary and middle school kids during that time we knew *had* to have them. I have to admit that some of them were pretty cute, but a pink pig for $32.00 and a clear case for the pig for another $8.00 was nuts! It was supposed to be "a collector item of high value," Kevin would say. We didn't believe this pink pig was going to make him a fortune, but he wanted it and so we told him that we would buy it for him when his dad got paid that week. He didn't like that answer. He became very anxious and was starting to go into that mode of feeling so distraught that he couldn't contain his emotions, that he could possibly lose that beanie baby. He was about to do the "fish flop" on the floor right in the middle of the store. The "fish flop," as we called it, was where he fell onto the floor and would begin crying uncontrollably while flopping around, saying out loud "Oh my God, Oh my God." He just couldn't get over the fact that the pig might be gone by the time we came back to purchase it and that someone else would get it. Apparently, there wasn't another one in the whole universe. It was that big of a deal to him, and we still have that pink pig in the special clear case keeping it in pristine condition. It was hard to know which battles to pick with Kevin, since his emotions were so intense and he had trouble regulating them. Often it was just exhausting and agreeing to spend a few dollars on something to avoid an overwhelming meltdown from him over and over again seemed to save a lot of trouble. We didn't have to resources at the time to understand what was going on, and sometimes we felt blind handling those situations. We were just doing what we felt was best for everyone at the time.

Eventually, McDonald's came out with their own set of Beanie Babies. There were four different types in their collection, and Kevin had to have them all. Some were difficult to get because they were the hot item to collect, and they sold out quickly. The last beanie baby for his collection became available one particular day, and he couldn't wait for school to be over with so that he could get the last one to complete his collection. That day we drove to several McDonald's to find it. He showed so much anxiety when it wasn't at the first McDonald's, and the second one, then finally we got it at the third McDonalds. He was so worked up about whether we would get it that day. He just couldn't relax. We did finally get the beanie baby that day, the one he needed to complete his collection, and his anxiety visibly improved. Of course, they were worth more money in the package, so he never played with them. He just collected them. He was happy, though, and that was very important.

Even with all of the Beanie Baby obsessions, he was still pursuing his interest in magic. He was still dabbling in coins and was starting to get interested in more tricks. He started with the Hot Rod trick. It's a rectangular plastic rod with colored rhinestones on two sides of the rod. Each week we would go to the magic shop to find something new for Kevin to learn. Once we bought the trick, the magician would teach Kevin how to perform it. Paul and I had to walk away from the counter so that we wouldn't see how the trick was done. Then Kevin would practice the trick at home, and when he thought he had perfected it, he would try it out on us. He was hugely interested in sponge ball illusions at the time he started and would sit on the floor in his bedroom in front of his mirrored closet doors and practice for hours. He was very persistent in having to practice his new craft, and it was amazing what he could do with those sponge balls. He fooled us all the time, and it was so fun to watch! He eventually became very good at magic tricks and started a YouTube channel online where he would demonstrate them.

EVERYTHING IS CHANGING AGAIN

It was January 2001 when Paul came home from work around 10:30 in the morning. I was so surprised to see him, and he looked very upset. He said he had been laid off work again. It was such a big blow to him, like getting kicked in the stomach, and it wasn't the first time it had happened. It was the fourth time in his twenty-two-year career at the Jet Propulsion Laboratory that he was laid off. The aerospace industry had been hit hard in the 1990's, and many highly-educated engineers had lost their jobs and had difficulty finding work afterward. Paul felt that no-one would hire him again, even though I knew that wasn't true at all. He was just depressed about the situation and feeling insecure at the time, which was understandable.

We didn't have any family that lived nearby, and we were having trouble with Kevin's behavior at home, so we thought about moving to Lake Havasu City, Arizona to be near my dad and stepmom. Paul and I thought that maybe they could help us with Kevin. He had been seeing a behavioral counselor, psychologist, and then a psychiatrist over the past couple of years, but was still very defiant, belligerent, and was hitting us and punching holes in walls and doors. When we finally decided to move, and the house was up for sale, Kevin kicked in his bedroom door. He was angry over who knows what? Maybe it was the move, but it could also be the littlest thing that would set him off into a rage.

We had been remodeling the house over the past two years and had transformed it from a house built in 1960 to an upgraded, beautiful home with style and décor of the year 2001. Once we put the house on the market, we got an offer within a couple of weeks. It was a full price offer, and we started packing up the house to move to Arizona. Escrow was moving along quickly, and before we knew it, we had left California. We loved living there, and were concerned about moving, but felt it was the best thing to do at that time for Kevin. We had to try something new. Thankfully, Paul was able to fix the door Kevin had kicked in before the house sold. Life had been very difficult for all of us, and it wasn't getting any better. Kevin was about to turn thirteen, and we hoped this change would be for the better, for all our sakes.

Paul and I really needed help with Kevin; we needed some family interaction from my dad and stepmom. Kevin needed to see his grandparents, and maybe they could have him over to their house for a weekend and spend some quality time with him. Maybe they would have a positive influence over him and could bond a little.

We were also hoping they would understand the difficulties we were having with him and the fact that they weren't caused by us spoiling him too much. They always thought that we did too much for him. Yes, Kevin was spoiled, but there was an equal amount of discipline and consequences delivered. There were serious issues going on with Kevin that we were struggling to handle and they weren't because he was spoiled at times. We were at a loss of how to get Kevin to behave, perform in school, and feel the happiness of living life. Ever since he was in the first grade, Kevin had feelings of wanting to die. He wrote notes and letters about how he hated his life and wished he were dead. Those letters were extremely concerning, and we reached out to so many professionals, but nothing was working. We were hoping that his grandparents could help in some way. There were days when we weren't sure that he would live to see his eighteenth birthday.

Kevin had a fun first summer in Lake Havasu. He learned to swim. Being thirteen and not knowing how to swim when you lived near a lake wasn't very safe or smart, but he did learn, and we were proud of him. Some milestones may seem small, perhaps, especially for the age he was when he learned certain things, but for us, these were the big ones.

When Kevin was around five years old, I took him for swimming lessons, but he had a bad experience. The lessons were held at various houses in the area in their backyard pools. There the trained instructors taught the kids how to swim. His instructor divided the class into two groups. One group was in the main pool, and the other group was in the jacuzzi awaiting their turn to work with the instructor. Kevin was sitting in the jacuzzi, and he slipped underneath the water. Just as I was walking up to the gate to pick him up from the class, I saw the instructor pull him up and out of the jacuzzi with one arm very quickly. This bad experience had a profound effect on him, and we weren't ever able to get him back in the pool for swimming lessons for many more years. He refused to go near the water after that. Now at thirteen, he was ready to try again. He did very well in class, and we were so proud of him. My Mom would say, "He swims like a fish now!" He had come so far, and now we could relax a little bit because he would be safe around the water.

That summer he also got to camping at the beach in San Diego, California. The YMCA put together a fantastic trip where they bussed about forty kids from Lake Havasu City to San Diego for a week. They slept right on the beach in these small tents and had a lot of fun.

In 2001, back when we were living in Lake Havasu City, Arizona, Kevin and his dad started a magic trick sales company called London Bridge Magic. Paul was hoping that Kevin would take an interest in the business and it would be an avenue for Kevin to focus his energies, instead of playing his Gemstone game online so much. Paul designed the website, and they both decided to go to the swap meet to sell their magic tricks. The first couple of times were fun. We were all awake at 5:00 a.m. to load up the van, drove to the swap meet and set up our booth. We never sold much, but it was fun watching Kevin perform the tricks and teach others how to do them. He would perform a trick and spike their interest, but they had to buy the trick first before Kevin would show them how it was done and help them practice it. Magicians say "showing someone one time is a trick, but more than once, that is a lesson." Soon the swap meet got to be old. It became miserable trying to get Kevin out of bed to go there, so we finished out the season, but never went back again. We sold what we could online, but still had a lot of inventory left over.

The summer finally came to a close, and it was time for Kevin to go back to school. Starting eighth grade at Dayton Middle School in Lake Havasu City, a new school in a new city must have been intimidating, but Kevin went off to school just fine and appeared as if everything was going to be alright. In the beginning, things were o.k., but eventually he started struggling again. We had a few days of him not wanting to go to school or do his homework. School was always a struggle. I would pick him up afterward, and he told me of some disturbing things the other kids would say and do. The kids were always cursing and talking about sex. Kevin was shy and was taken aback by the way they talked. They were rude and crude, and he found that middle school was much rougher than elementary school. Soon he didn't want to go to school at all. He was always tardy, and that was if I could get him to school at all.

The time came where we decided that there needed to be another school evaluation of Kevin. We had been down this road many times, but this time was a little different. The school officials observed him during class and when leaving class. They found out the other kids were bullying him when leaving class and going to the next one, that they were downright mean. The principal called us in for a meeting to discuss what to do with Kevin. I thought, *what to do with Kevin?* It is clear the bullies needed to receive some form of punishment. Kevin wasn't asking to be bullied. The teachers and principal told us that they couldn't keep him safe at their school. They wouldn't always be around to monitor the kids when changing classrooms, and they didn't feel they could keep him safe, and that it was in our best interest to move Kevin to another school. That was quite shocking to hear.

We didn't know whether to be angry with the staff for wanting to get him out of their school or thankful that they were truthful with us about his safety and their concerns. *Can't Kevin catch a break in life?* My thoughts swirled, and questions followed me around day and night. *Why does he have to struggle so much?* He didn't do anything to cause those kids to bully him. *Why do some kids have to be so mean? Bullying has to stop!* Now, more than ever, I realize that it's something that has a profound effect on a child's future and how they handle situations or crisis' in life. Bullying hurts them to the core of their being.

He was transferred to Thunderbolt Middle School for the second, third, and fourth quarters to complete his eighth-grade classes. It ended up being a positive move. He had another psychological evaluation in January of 2002, and the school psychologist found that Kevin did qualify for Special Education services with the categorical eligibility of "Emotional Disability." "*The conclusion of this assessment was Kevin's achievement scores were within normal limits. He has been very unsuccessful in the regular classroom setting without Special Education support and instruction. Socially, Kevin has not developed interpersonal relationships with his peers. The results of the current behavior rating scales indicate that Kevin has exhibited the following emotional problems, over an extended period, and to such a degree as to significantly interfere with his educational progress in the following areas:*

-An inability to establish or maintain satisfactory interpersonal relationships with peers, parents or teachers.

-An inability to learn which cannot be explained by intellectual, sensory, or other health factors.

-The general pervasive mood of unhappiness or depression.
It is determined that Kevin <u>does</u> meet the specific criteria for eligibility for Special Education services, with the categorical eligibility of Emotional Disability."

Hearing these words made us cry. We wished Kevin didn't have to struggle so much in life. It was so hard to hear and read of our son's problems, but we knew they were there, and we were so grateful for this psychologist to intervene and provide Kevin with the support he would need when transitioning into high school the following year.

When Kevin entered the ninth grade at Lake Havasu High School in September of 2002, the class had an assignment to write a Self-Concept Inner Portrait. I was so impressed when I read it, and it still surprises me today. He had come such a long way in his development. I'm still so proud of him and of what he wrote.

Self-Concept Inner Portrait
09/09/2002

"Self-image is the way you look at yourself. To start, many people have influenced my self-concept including my mom, and my dad. I will include how each of these people in my life greatly improved my life and my self-esteem. My dad always said, "There is no try, only do," and, "Try isn't a word, it's what I do is what counts." I have noticed that if I say, "I will, instead of, "I can," I am more successful, especially in school. It has done wonderfully. My mom also helps me by motivating me when I do get good grades, which, of course, helps. My mom and my family have always told me, "You can put your mind to anything you want to," and thus, it has been successful, especially in school. I did exactly that, and now my grades are improving, and I'm getting A's and B's in most subjects!

What influenced my self-esteem most was, as I said, my parents. Why did I go back to studying and getting good grades? Well quite obviously, I felt good about my self-image, and my self-esteem was raised higher and higher every day as I said, "I will do this, I will ace this test!" repeated over and over. I am confident in myself. People's insults do not bother me; nor do their harassments. When you're truly confident in yourself, you don't care what other people's "opinions" are, and about how "bad" they think you are, it doesn't matter. That's when you realize that it's "your" opinion that counts. Other people's insulting or mentally harmful opinions mean nothing. Also, through my study of psychology, people who put-down people; they do it because they do feel bad about themselves to a degree. They also feel bad about their self-image.

How I handle positive influences events in my life: I use them to the best of my ability. For example, since I have study hall in the sixth period, I always take that time to study to the best of my ability, and to study hard. All I can say is it's paid off, compared to all the other kids there just playing around and practically doing nothing, just talking and chatting, claiming they don't have "any" homework when they do. I have improved a lot over the course of a year, I got very angry about small things, (not being able to go to the soda machine after school, etc.) and I broke into outrages, which has now been reduced best as possible to a minimum. I did not handle this healthy in the past, but I do now. I have now learned to control it, by taking deep breaths and doing anger management exercises, etc. Writing out my feelings, going outside and playing with my dogs, or taking a walk. These things have helped me get control of my unhealthy methods of coping, for example: hitting things, punching holes in walls, and kicking in doors. Those things are not healthy ways of coping with life.

Everyone's childhood is most likely based on your future to some degree. For example, if you learned to put-down people by words, then it would eventually lead to more severe incidents, (fights, sometimes suspension, etc.). So basically, what is learned in your childhood is most likely going to carry on with you to your high school.

Childhood experiences − When kids tease you at home or school, it can hurt your feelings, and change the way you feel about yourself. You might start believing what those kids say is true, but it's only a poor self-image that makes one feel that way.

The good experiences in childhood also impact one's life. Like learning Karate at an early age, also playing soccer, having friends to be around with, collecting rocks, coins, and beanie babies and learning all about them. Every experience determines one's sense of self − the good and the bad.

Messages of self-talk − think positive, try my best and help others succeed. I feel good about myself when I help others." Written by, Kevin Tejan

It was such beautiful writing, a Self-Concept Inner Portrait of himself. It was insightful, caring, honest, and very revealing. It was a window into his soul; his soul who has been through a lot in his short fourteen years of life. We hoped that this would be a real turning point for Kevin in the way he understood himself, and the world around him.

BEHAVIORAL HEALTH ISSUES – WHAT THE HECK IS HAPPENING?

It was now 2003, and just when we thought life had smoothed out, something new happened. Kevin had a nice summer break and was always online playing a game called Gemstone. He became obsessed with it and would play till all hours of the night through the morning. It was summer break, so we didn't mind too much. When he entered the 10th grade, his grades were mostly A's, B's and a couple of C's. It appeared that he was having a better academic school year than in years past. In fact, he was honored by the Rotary Club of Lake Havasu Sunrise Group in his Sophomore year for the recognition of his devotion to attain a high scholastic level while participating in activities which develop good citizenship. The Rotary Club presented Kevin with a fifty-dollar check and a certificate at one of their monthly breakfast meetings. Then they took his picture for the newspaper. It was more exciting to Paul and I, we were so proud of him, but Kevin just went through the motions of having to be there at the presentation. You could tell that he was very uncomfortable when being recognized at the breakfast and was having a hard time looking happy or smiling.

It was an awkward time in a teenager's life, and Kevin was struggling. Not long after the award was given, on August 18, 2003, we found a note on his computer. He must have been posting on the Gemstone game forum and looking for help. He wrote:

"Can you answer this, please? I don't know what's wrong with me. I think I have depression, everyday thoughts of suicide drift into my mind, and I think about it every

day. I am very hostile with my parents, and only around them, never to strangers. I get "flashes" of information like for example me in a school shooting and killing everyone. I wouldn't actually do this, but it drifts into my mind. I can't control what drifts in. Almost all the time I think of dying, and I have too many problems. Most times if I had a handgun next to me I would kill myself.

I go to a psychiatrist, and he isn't very helpful. I tell him things he says it'll be private, then he sends me out of the room, and later my parents tell me that what I said to him, he told them. My parents think I have ADD, ADHD, and depression. I KNOW I have depression, and I take medication for it. I also had ticks, but the medicine is controlling that. My medicine has NO effect on my depression. I really need help here, please."

"Also, I forgot to say, I tell them I'd commit suicide (and I would) but they don't listen. They say "Whatever" or "Go ahead," I think they're sarcastic. Before I told my psychiatrist about my problems and he said it was serious and I needed to go to a mental hospital. So, yes, they threw me in a mental hospital for two weeks. It was awful. Now I'm afraid that anything I say, (Like I'm going to kill myself) to him, he'll just go ahead and send me back. I don't want that! Please help. -Kevin

Someone named Lucie responded, and she said she was concerned about him and wanted Kevin to get better.

"You seem scared, hurt and confused. All of those feelings are easy to understand. I'd like to help by connecting you with new people you would feel safe to talk with about your thoughts and feelings. You deserve this care.

This helpful group is part of the National Suicide Hotline (1-800-SUICIDE), a 24/7 confidential crisis support line answered by knowledgeable staff, trained and willing to help. Please call.

You'll be in my thoughts." – Lucie

Finding this on our son's computer was extremely concerning. It wasn't the first time that Kevin had expressed these types of feelings, but this note was more advanced this time, as far as the expression of his feelings. His dad and I were so sad and scared to know that he was still struggling and that nothing really appeared to be helpful for him. We had tried counseling, medicine, prayer, church, discipline, no discipline, lots of talking, crying, compromise, encouragement, and yet he was still struggling with life in so many areas. He wasn't happy.

One afternoon, when we were still living in Lake Havasu, Kevin had just finished a counseling session, and we were going to dinner somewhere that he didn't want to go. Instead, Kevin wanted to go directly home so he could play his Gemstone game. Since he wasn't getting his way and was angry about it, Kevin jumped out of our truck while it was moving, rolled on the ground and ran off towards home. My heart jumped out of my chest; it was shocking to see him do something like that. He didn't appear to be hurt when he jumped out, so we let him walk towards home. We figured that he needed some time to cool off and hopefully think about what he had done and how it wasn't the smartest thing to do.

It wasn't the first time he had thrown a fit in the car. We were headed somewhere, and Kevin needed new batteries for one of his hand-held games. He was so angry that we wouldn't stop at a store immediately to buy batteries, that he threw the bad batteries at Paul while he was driving. They hit the front windshield making a very loud sound. We thought for sure the windshield had cracked, but it hadn't. The only thing we could think to do was to keep driving and stay calm. It wasn't going to do any good to yell and scream at him. Trying to reason with him didn't work when he was in this unreasonable state of mind. We just tried to diffuse the situation.

Much of Kevin's anger surrounded him handling stress, gaming systems, and not getting what he wanted at the moment. Paul tried blocking the Gemstone website and put in a monitoring system that limited the amount of time he could spend on the computer, and also the times he could access his game. If it wasn't us trying to control the time he was on the computer, it was the gaming trolls, teasing him and sending him into rages or deep sadness and depression. The game controlled his emotions.

Oftentimes when playing his Gemstone game, Kevin would get incredibly angry; so much so that he ended up kicking in his bedroom door. At first, the hole was small, but after more angry times on the computer, the hole was so big that you could just crawl through it. That's when we just took his door off the hinges. He didn't get a door anymore. We knew that the door would have to be replaced eventually. After time passed, we hoped he would get over wanting to hit doors, but he didn't. He ended up kicking in his bathroom door and punched holes all down the hallway.

We were staying at a house that belonged to my dad and step-mom when all of this was happening, waiting until we were ready to purchase our own house. The pressure was on to repair it perfectly, and thankfully Paul was so handy fixing everything.

I don't think we ever told my parents about the hallway and doors. It's a good thing that they had their own house in Havasu Springs (about a half hour away), and sometimes they were at their other home in Kentucky. Most of the time when my parents were in town, we were able to arrange seeing them at a restaurant. We didn't want them to see any of the destruction Kevin had done to their house. We knew how sick it would make them feel, and we didn't want them to think badly about their grandson.

On another occasion, Kevin used a knife or something sharp and wrote on the bathroom mirror some bad stuff, and I tried to clean it off with Scrubbing Bubbles, hoping to rub out some of the lighter scratches. I learned the hard way that I had left the cleaning product on too long, and it etched off the surface of the mirror. This bathroom mirror was humongous. It was an L-shaped mirror that went from the countertop all the way up to the ceiling. We ended up replacing the entire mirror without his grandparents ever knowing what Kevin had done. All of this was due to his Obsessive-Compulsive Disorder, his anger outbursts, and not being able to handle stress, among all of the other things going on inside his head.

Kevin was now entering eleventh grade at Lake Havasu High School, and we were gearing up for another school year. From the first day, it was a rough start. He wouldn't even get out of bed to go to school most mornings. We met with the school officials, and they suggested a self-paced computer-based school for Kevin, and recommended Desert Technology High School, and we enrolled him there.

At first, Kevin was excited to go to this school because of the computers. He completed all of his school work online, and since he was very fast at keyboarding, he had an edge over the other students who weren't as fast. The school allowed students to bring in their own CD player to listen to music while they worked. He liked this too, but unfortunately, his CD player was stolen one day. He was pretty shocked and disillusioned that someone would steal something from someone. He must have been feeling like he was being bullied again because things changed after that event, and it was increasingly difficult to get him to go to school. It became a fight to get him there almost every day. His depression and anger outbursts were more extreme than ever, and we were getting worried that he wouldn't graduate high school on time. We became increasingly worried about his mental health, as the state it was in wasn't improving either.

In November 2004, Kevin was sixteen years old, and was angry over something. Possibly having to do his homework, or maybe take a shower; it was hard to know for sure, since it didn't take much for him to go into a rage. This particular night Kevin was very angry, and walked out the front door, threw a rock at our front living room window and broke it.

We didn't know what to do with him. He was continually acting out, and it was mostly unexpected. His reactions rarely seemed to match the situation of why he was upset a particular time. After a while, he came back inside the house and was still upset with himself, his dad and me, and he lashed out and kicked me. I told him to stop it, or we would have to call the police. I figured he would calm down, but he didn't. He kicked me again. This time it was on purpose, just to make a point that he wanted to go to jail. He was always saying that going to jail would solve his problems in life. He thought a mental hospital or jail was the answer. He was insisting on having me call the police so he kicked me again on purpose so I would do so. I didn't want to bring the police into the situation, but as a parent I knew I had to set an example by following through with what I said I would do. I called the police, and they came over to the house and carted him off to jail for a couple of hours. They were going to admit him to the Kingman Behavioral Hospital but felt it was too rough for him to be in that facility, so they called us to come pick him up.

They did file a police report, and Kevin had to meet with a Probation Officer and discuss his situation and apologize for it. The officer gave him community service. Kevin was required to perform twelve hours of community service to clean up a park. Then he had to attend six sessions of counseling for anger management and write two essays. The first essay was to develop a Safety Plan for when he feels like he wants to do something bad. A plan to decide what he would do, who would he call, and how would he act the next time. The second essay was a short-term, midterm, and a long-term goal plan for his future. Kevin acted as if it was a stupid meeting and no big deal at all. At the time, it didn't appear that his punishment had affected him much at all.

Then, five days later I found this suicide note in his room and realized that meeting with the Probation Officer did have some effect on him, and it wasn't positive.

He wrote – *"I just want to die. Sometimes we all just want to die, and just sit down and cry. All day and all night I feel this way; as no one cares, it's just no one knows how I feel. I would kill to feel better, and that's probably what I'll do is kill myself, boo-hoo. All he does is cry and whine. That kid will never do it. I'll show you when you see me dead next to your door.*

If people cared, they would help. Like that juvenile justice lady, she thinks that giving me twelve hours of community service is going to help me. Ha-ha, wouldn't be funny if I killed myself there? You know, I hope I f...ing die before the deadline, cause if I don't, I'll do it in prison. Try me. F.... ing B...ch. Then I hope they get their goddamn ASS sued. And I hope to hell and back I'll be over every goddamn news channel in

Arizona. And all the b.... ches and fa...ots that doubted me or humiliated me cry their little eyes until they go to hell. For anyone who supported me...thanks."

"Whoever is reading this, you can doubt me all you want. But I promise you this: In the end, I <u>will</u> kill myself."

Plan A.

-Bullet caliber between 0.8 and .25mm

-Sturdy makeshift slingshot with rubber band

-Small flat-nosed nail

-Put a bullet to head. Take nail and place nose of the nail on the primer of the round. Take strong slingshot rubber bands (short) and put the nail in the slingshot so when released distance elapsed as short as possible for maximum pressure and release it so the head of the nail drives into the primer hard; round will explode.

Plan B.

-Hang

Plan C.

-Use a high caliber pistol (magnum) revolver. Place barrel end on the temple. Pull trigger.

Plan D.

-Suicide by cop, if all else fails.

I was so worried when I read this and brought the note to the officer looking for some help or some more counseling sessions for Kevin. She called me later that day and said she had to do a welfare check on him and send Child Protective Services to the house. I said "That would be great, I'm willing to take all of the help I can get." My child was hurting, and we hadn't figured out how to help him. The woman I spoke with called back and said that if we could get Kevin to the Mohave County Mental Health Department right then, she wouldn't have to send CPS to our house. We went right away to meet with a "Screener" at the Mohave County Mental Health Department Crisis Center for an evaluation on whether he would hurt himself right then and needed admittance to the hospital. The counselor we met with talked with Kevin and me; then she left the room for a few minutes, and when she returned she said that Kevin only needed counseling, and then said we would receive a bill for this one visit. It was a strange, out of the blue comment, because we weren't even talking about an invoice. We thought she was leaving the room to get more help. It's as if she didn't hear anything or didn't know what to do either. It became clearer when she said that we made too much money and didn't qualify for their services, and that was all they could do for us. There we went again falling between the cracks and not getting help. That wasn't anything new. She gave me names of a couple of counselors, and we left and went home. The Probation Officer just had to go through the motions because I brought her the suicide note, and she had to follow through with CPS or a counselor. Again, no real help.

Kevin did see a Psychologist when we first moved to Lake Havasu. LD. Lumpkin worked with Kevin for a few months until he said that he couldn't do anything else for Kevin unless he was willing to take the steps and do the work that they discussed in their sessions. Dr. Lumpkin said he didn't feel it was worth it to keep meeting with Kevin, as he would basically just be taking our money for nothing. He released Kevin and said he could come back when he was ready to act on his words to get better. I appreciated the doctor's honesty and knew he had Kevin's best interest at heart. Kevin had been going there for several months, and nothing was changing for him. I think this was a little push from the doctor to get Kevin to react and take some action – which was o.k.

He also saw a psychiatrist because he was on medications and needed to continue them, so he started seeing Dr. Kaperonis, a psychiatrist in Lake Havasu City. In the beginning, it seemed their visits went well. Dr. Kaperonis diagnosed him with Major Depression, Bipolar Disorder, and numerous learning disabilities. We were happy with the doctor, and Kevin seemed to open up to him in their sessions. Towards the end of December 2001, the doctor wanted a second opinion on Kevin's diagnosis, because of his increasing outbursts at home and his obsessive behavior to play his online Gemstone game. He was hitting me and punching holes in walls, self-mutilating (cutting marks on his legs) and making threats to kill himself as well as voicing suicidal ideation. He wasn't responding to outpatient treatment and intensive medication management. Kevin had a recent episode of holding a knife to his throat. He felt it was important for Kevin to go to Monte Vista Hospital in Las Vegas, Nevada for an evaluation. Kevin was there from December 12, 2001 through December 22, 2001.

Deciding to admit Kevin to a psychiatric hospital for ten days was a huge step. I think it was scary for Kevin, his dad and myself. I'll never forget driving him to Las Vegas and meeting with the doctors at his intake appointment. Paul and I were answering the doctor's questions, and another person came up to us and said he was there to take Kevin's belongings. He asked Kevin to take off his shoes and remove his shoelaces. It had never dawned on us that patients there would consider using shoelaces to hurt themselves. We were entering a different type of world that we never thought we would be a part of. At the hospital, Kevin attended group sessions with the other patients, and heard about their problems and issues also. When we visited, he told us some wild stories that were entertaining to hear, but very sad. One patient was hallucinating by seeing things on the walls and freaking out. Another was there because she witnessed a murder and was very distraught. There was one patient who was screaming, and the staff couldn't calm her down, so they sedated her with Haldol and locked her up in a room by herself where she had to sleep it off the next day. We felt lucky that Kevin didn't have to deal with those types of problems.

During his time there, he learned coping skills. He attended classes, participated in discussion groups, and journaled his thoughts. They gave him workbooks to complete, to log his feelings for the day, and he earned school credit for the two weeks he was there. Some of his coping skills were to count to ten and take a deep breath to calm his emotions down, take a walk outside and chill by walking away from a situation where he was feeling angry or sad, listen to music on the radio, and play with his dogs. Play video games and go to sleep. Thinking positively, by doing well, and by listening well. Those were the skills Kevin decided that he could manage.

Kevin was at the hospital for ten very long days. It was a long time to be away from him. He had never been out of our sight in all these years; he didn't even have a babysitter. Occasionally, his grandmother would watch him for a few hours or a rare couple of days, but that was it. After the ten days of evaluation, the doctors didn't tell us anything new that we didn't already know. They said, "he has a social skills deficit, due to prematurity and some neurological dysfunctions, OCD and self-esteem problems – was fragile when things didn't go his way." Because of his addiction to the text based online game, the doctor said that he would probably be a good programmer someday.

It was frustrating that the doctors didn't notice there was a problem with the online gaming and the issue wasn't being addressed. In essence, nothing helpful came from his ten days stay at this mental health facility.   Dr. Kaperonis was content that the visit confirmed his treatment was on track, but we didn't feel there was any progress or solution for Kevin or us.

We were just happy that he was being discharged just a couple of days before Christmas. We really missed him and wanted him back with us. Paul and I picked him up from the hospital and drove straight to my mom's house in Morongo Valley, which is near Palm Springs, California. We were all happy to be together again, and we had a nice Christmas there.

GROWING UP WITH MANY ANIMALS

At one point, we had three dogs and twenty-seven rabbits. How and why did we have twenty-seven rabbits? Well, we originally had only one rabbit named Rocky who was an Easter present. When I was homeschooling him back in California, I said to Kevin, if he wanted to do a report on the gestation of rabbits, we could get a female and have ONE litter. So, we got Butterscotch for Rocky. They loved each other so much, and very quickly, Kevin was able to report on the fact that it takes only thirty-one days and you'll have baby bunnies! Later on, when we lived in Lake Havasu, the Humane Society discovered that we had a lot of rabbits and truly loved them, so they would call us if they had a rabbit that had to be euthanized because no one had adopted him or her yet. Of course, we wouldn't let that happen, so we would happily take the rabbit home with us. We took in four or five rabbits that way. I guess the rabbits all loved each other very much because at one point we ended up with twenty-seven of them! They were our pets, and we could never think of giving any of them away, especially when we heard that there were a lot of snake owners in Lake Havasu who liked to feed the rabbits to them.

The rabbits were time-consuming; it took a lot of time to clean up after them and play with each of them. We would sit in front of the television and hold several bunnies at a time and would rotate them out on different nights. They did get a lot of attention from all of us; however, Kevin thought his dad loved the rabbits more than him, and he became resentful of the rabbits. This became deadly later on.

It was a constant roller coaster with Kevin. He sure kept us on our toes, but we were up for the challenge to provide him with a happy, healthy life. I just wished that sometimes he didn't make it so hard on us.

One night in the spring of 2004, while we were living in Lake Havasu City, Paul and I had gone to bed, and Kevin decided to play with matches. He purposely burned off the two ferrets' whiskers and large patches of hair on their backs, and then burned a hole in one of the ferrets' stomach area. We also had a couple of rabbits inside the house in a cage and noticed that their ears looked odd. Looking closer at their ears, we found they were sticky, and one ear was half-chewed off, and the other ear had a hunk taken out of it, and they smelled sweet like Kahlua. When we noticed the ferrets and rabbits, we questioned Kevin about their condition. It was hard to believe that he would hurt them, but he had. It was troubling to us that Kevin didn't think he was doing anything wrong. He did apologize and went on with his day as if it wasn't that big of an event. He had to have known that what he was doing was wrong. You don't just burn an animal or put Kahlua on a rabbits' ears. The ferrets were special to him. He always gave them so much attention, and they were so cute. They were his pets. I can't imagine why he would hurt them, it never made any sense. What on earth was going through his teenage brain?

Later that same evening, Kevin asked me if I still loved him. I said "Yes, I still love you. I love you unconditionally, and always will no matter what." Then he said to me, "Would you still love me if I murdered someone?" I paused and then said, "Yes, I would still love you. I would be very disappointed in you and heartbroken if you were to do anything as cruel as that." I was trying so hard to stay calm, so as to not draw attention to what appeared to be a question where he was fishing for a reaction out of me. What was going through his mind? We needed help with him. We needed help badly, but it felt as though we had exhausted every option. It was getting scary living with him at times, and we started locking our bedroom door most nights.

Paul and I thought back a few years and realized that there were three other instances where he had hurt animals that we had forgotten. The first time he squeezed his mouse, Brittany. He said he wanted to see how it felt. He was only six years old at the time. We made him apologize to Brittany and say a prayer for her, then he dropped her in the trash can and walked away like it was nothing. He wasn't affected by what he had done. We were more disturbed by his unfeeling actions than anything else. The second time was when he pulled at our Sheltie's hair, and he turned and bit Kevin's lip. They were together in Kevin's bedroom, and we were in the other room. This dog was very calm and very even-tempered. I can't imagine that he would react that way, but he did, and it must have been serious because the dog bit his lip enough to where Kevin needed stitches. The third time he threw down my Maltese, Cricket, so hard that it broke his leg and possibly his back, and we had to put him to sleep. That was my dog. I was so mad at Kevin for hurting him, and I made sure he understood how wrong it was and how sad it made me feel. I made Kevin go with me to the Orange County Humane Shelter to bring Cricket there to get put to sleep. He needed to see what the result of his actions had done to an innocent animal. Eventually, Kevin apologized for getting so angry that he threw Cricket down and he realized it was wrong. Nevertheless, my Cricket was gone forever.

FORTY DAYS AT REALITY
RANCH BOOT CAMP

Paul and I were really at a loss of how and what we needed to do to handle Kevin. We were at our wits end. We thought it would be a good idea to send Kevin to a boot camp to learn motivation and self-discipline, and to develop a greater appreciation for his home and family. It had been very stressful and rough living with him up to that point. He didn't do anything we asked and was extremely argumentative and defiant. His psychiatrist didn't think it was the right kind of discipline for Kevin there either, but we sent him there anyway. To us, this camp was a solution to shipping him into shape. His Grandpa Walker wanted to pay for it. It cost $4000, and he thought it was something that would be good for Kevin also. He always thought that we didn't discipline Kevin enough and were too easy on him. His grandpa just never knew how bad things were and what Kevin had done to the walls and doors and mirrors of his Lake Havasu City home.

We were all hopeful that some good would come from this boot camp. Kevin was sixteen, and that July we drove him to Phoenix Sky Harbor Airport to meet the group that was going to Reality Camp via bus. There were about 30-40 other boys attending the camp. They loaded the kids onto a bus for a two-hour drive to Snowflake and Concho located in the White Mountains of Northern Arizona near Show Low.

The campers wrote us weekly to tell us how things were going. Kevin's first letter was as follows:

10 things that I will change while at this camp:

1. Gain integrity, change how much I take for granted such as TV, Radio, music and my coin collection. Unfortunately, we don't realize this until it is too late.
2. To become more in-shape and continue to be physically active upon my return
3. Another value I would change is to stop acting "strange" around my peers. I set myself up for trouble: for attention.
4. Control my lust towards adolescent females
5. Control my anger towards my elders and peers
6. Control my profanity
7. Control my diet at home
8. Gain a lot of self-control from this camp. I would use it to my advantage at school.
9. I would also be nicer to animals. I should use the golden rule on them.
10. And finally, I would raise my self-esteem, so I feel happier. It feels horrid to feel depressed. The more self-esteem you have, the happier you feel. I hope this camp   will change me in that aspect.

Second letter – This camp is tough, the first week is called "hell week." It is hard, all we do is PT (physical training). No showers, only deodorant, and the food is really bad. All we eat are grits, tuna, spaghetti, and nasty oatmeal. They make us lick our plates. We only get water to drink while the sergeants are popping open soda cans. I miss you mom and dad, and Spunky (his ferret).

Third letter – How are you doing? This camp really sucks. The sergeants sing dirty songs. It's funny but really bad. We went into Show Low and ate at a Mexican restaurant and went bowling. One day I was supposed to be picking up trash with another camper, and we sat down, so they made us carry a damn tree everywhere we went that day.

Fourth letter – This letter is about why I came here. I came here because my parents don't seem to discipline me enough and I have problems controlling my anger, and because I cuss at my parents. Another reason I came here is: I want to be healthier and to get into better shape. It's hard for me to run since I'm overweight, I mostly walk and run. I used to be addicted to an online game called Gemstone III, so my parents terminated the game. I came here to gain discipline, confidence, self-esteem, motivation, and to get fit.

Fifth letter – How are you doing? I really hate this camp. I accidentally left my canteen by my cot, and when I came back it was gone. Now I have no water, and no one wants to share their canteen. I hope I find my canteen or I get another one. Some of the kids here have pissed in their canteens. I'm not sure I want to drink out of that. Due to a camper doing that, they took our showers down. I have now realized how spoiled I am, and how much I took for granted. Soon we will play paintball and climb a mountain. I am looking forward to this.

Final letter – August 2004, I believe this is my last essay. This essay/letter is about what I did wrong to arrive at this camp. Before I came to this camp, I've had problems with anger. I would break down doors, hit my parents, and cuss at them. I also took way too much for granted. I had had depression and suicide thoughts before I came here as well.

I take medication for it. Before I was sent here, I was sent to a mental hospital. There I learned how to control my anger better, and I learned a lot about depression. When I came back home, I acted more motivated, and my behavior had improved. However, after about a year I began to cuss at them more. They warned me I would be sent to a military camp. A few years later, they sent me here.

Mom and Dad, I'm sorry about how I've treated you. When I come home in a week, I will not swear at you anymore, and I will impress you on how my behavior has improved. When I lie on my bed when I come home, I will appreciate how much I really do have instead of what I don't have.

It was nice to read the letters each week and see some progress in his attitude and behavior as the weeks went on, although we missed him very much and were looking forward to picking him up at the airport where we had dropped him off forty days earlier.

When we picked him up, we were shocked at how different he was! His physique had changed so much that we almost didn't recognize him. He was in fantastic shape and looked great! We were all excited to see each other, and the first thing he said was "Can I please have a soda?" We took him to eat at Kentucky Fried Chicken, and he got his large soda. He said it was the best meal he had in a long time. All in all, we thought this had been a good experience for him, but later on, he opened up to us and told us more of what happened there at camp.

He had some bad experiences that he hadn't written about. He said he couldn't write about them because the staff reviewed their letters before they mailed them, and he said he would be in a lot of trouble and would be punished, like having to carry a tree around all day, or some form of discipline if he said certain things. It reminds me of a boy's club where you wouldn't want to narc on your so-called friends or there would be hell to pay. When I found that out, I was angry with the instructors. They were supposed to be teachers and mentors to these troubled kids, and I just expected more from the staff. Maybe I was the naïve one here, but it sure didn't make me happy. I'm just glad he came home safe. Would we send him there again? No. It wasn't the right type of discipline that Kevin needed. This psychiatrist was right after all.

LEARNING TO DRIVE

Our baby wasn't a baby anymore. He was growing up too fast. Kevin was almost seventeen now, and he said that he wanted to learn how to drive. He had driven my brother's motorcycle before, and he did well. His dad was very surprised how it seemed so natural to him when shifting gears. We weren't ready to buy a motorcycle for him since it wasn't safe enough. In my mind, the perfect transportation would be some kind of floating bubble, or maybe a Hummer. I wanted my baby protected. Kevin had driven his motorized scooter around town and his bicycle, and now he wanted to drive a car. It's a turning point in every parent's life when your child wants to start driving, but I guess it had to come up sometime. We knew things were difficult for Kevin in many ways, but we still never knew exactly what the problem was. There wasn't a name for it except Depression and Obsessive-Compulsive Disorder (OCD). We hoped that with learning to drive and gaining some independence and confidence, he would start to enjoy life more in general.

We were still living in Lake Havasu City, and I remember taking him to the Motor Vehicle Department (MVD) for the first time to take his written test, and he failed it. I felt so bad for him, and he was so disappointed. I told him "Well, it was your first try, you'll pass the next time." After the test, he was telling me that he didn't understand some of the questions. I mentioned this to the examiner when they graded his test, and they told us that they offer a service to help people with special needs. We knew he had special needs and they said he just needed to schedule an appointment with an MVD specialist. She would read the questions out loud to him, and if he didn't understand it, he could ask for clarification. The point of the specialist was to make sure he understood the question before answering, and it made all the difference. He needed this extra help; all through his school years, he had trouble comprehending things and would ask a lot of questions. I'm sure his teachers felt he was a challenging student, but that was

Kevin. He was used to asking for clarification, and it worked - he passed his written test! He was so excited, and we were so proud of him. I know he was really proud of himself too at that moment. He accomplished a grown-up task.

Now came the scary part...driving with him at the wheel. With his learner's permit, Kevin drove around town with us, practicing for his driving test. We thought he was very good at driving. He practiced for a few months before taking the driving portion of the test. It helped build his confidence, and he passed the test the very first time. I could tell that he was very proud of himself. He was happy, smiling from ear to ear.

MOVING TO A LARGER CITY

It seemed that everything we tried to do for Kevin or help him with was an uphill battle. He had been to numerous behavioral counselors, psychologists, psychiatrists and was taking medication for his depression and obsessive-compulsive disorder. We exposed him to the piano, Karate, Taekwondo, tennis, soccer, basketball, baseball, summer camps, arts and crafts, and drama class at school. Out of all those, his favorite was Taekwondo, and he was very good at it. He was also still very fond of learning magic tricks. We were continually looking for something that he would connect with, that would enable us to find him the help he needed so desperately. His mental state of mind wasn't getting better. He was still struggling with life, and we had exhausted all the doctors in Lake Havasu City. Paul and I decided it was time to move to a larger city with more developmental services, and a larger pool of doctors to see if we could get the right help for Kevin.

In March 2005, we moved to Surprise, Arizona. It was about fifty miles west of Phoenix. Kevin had just turned seventeen, and we enrolled him in E-Institute, a public school that provided a self-paced learning environment with computers to complete his school work. Kevin loved to type, so this was right up his alley. E-Institute was a life saver. They were patient with him, and he did well there. He was known for his inquisitive nature and received a certificate for his inquisitiveness in one of his classes that same year. He must have liked it more than the other schools because I didn't have much trouble getting him up in the morning and getting to school on time. That was a nice change.

I can't remember what triggered him during one particular rage shortly after, but he was kicking me and yelling, and stabbing himself with a pocket knife. We called 911, and the police, fire trucks, and ambulances came right away. There was a knock at the door and standing in the doorway was the biggest and tallest officer I think I have ever seen. He was very calm and came inside the house and had

Kevin sit down on the stairs, and he just talked with him. He was able to get Kevin to calm down and agree to go with him to the hospital. Kevin was very cooperative, and they took him to the hospital by ambulance.

I think every neighbor was out on the street watching what was going on. It was quite a spectacle with three or four police cars, two fire engines, and two ambulances taking up the entire street. We had just moved into the neighborhood there in Surprise, Arizona, two months earlier, and our neighbors were probably wondering what kind of new neighbors they had in us. It was embarrassing, but necessary. Kevin was struggling, and we were looking for answers to get him help. Kevin being taken away in an ambulance was a "first" for all of us. The police told us we could go to the emergency room to meet up with him and talk to the doctors. When we arrived, there were social workers waiting to talk to us to find out what was going on with Kevin, and if anything like this had happened before. The doctors wanted to know what medicine he was currently taking, and the hospital asked us about our insurance. We were new in the area and didn't have any insurance, so they handed us a clipboard of papers to fill out so they could get us onto the state AHCCCS insurance program. Everything was moving so fast, and we felt like we were in a whirlwind tunnel wondering what was next. What were we supposed to do? They evaluated him and decided to transport him to a behavioral health hospital for further evaluation over the next two days until he was stable and could take him home.

The same thing happened again a few months later, and we knew what to expect by then. They would observe Kevin for 24-48 hours and then release him, once they thought he wasn't a harm to himself or others. When something awful like this happens to your family, the doctors point you in the direction where there is help in the way of counseling, social workers, and support for the family if we needed help in transporting him to and from his appointments. We were now "in the behavioral health system." We thought this could be a good thing to be able to get Kevin the help he so desperately needed. Unfortunately, there weren't many facilities near Surprise. Most of them were closer to the Phoenix area which was fifty miles away. *Should we move again?* We asked ourselves this a lot over the following weeks and months, but we knew we couldn't. We had just purchased a home and needed to look for services closer to where we lived. There had to be something, so we decided to keep trying.

Paul and I kept finding suicide notes in Kevin's room, and had many discussions with him trying to help him find some happiness and peace. We would talk with him about his feelings and would try to calm him down and work through his fears that life wasn't worth living. I'm glad that he would open up to me and that we could talk about how he felt.

Some of his notes read:

2005 - I really don't care about my parents paying for the funeral, its money. I don't think it's fair for counselors and psychiatrists to charge for their service. If someone is desperate, it should be free.

-Well, today is Monday. I've had yet another depression day, and I don't see how I'm going to live life to finish college. I want to get a Ph.D. in physics and then kill myself. And have people remorse about how smart I was. At least then, I'd be remembered.

-There's a train out in front of where I work at Fazoli's restaurant. If I could somehow manage to stand in front of the train when it's coming, that'd be a brutal way to die. I might do it though.

-I'm hoping to buy a handgun, but I'd have to wait until I'm 21. Maybe I could become a cop and shoot myself. Now, that'd make headlines. "Cop shoots himself."

-Shortly after moving to Surprise, Kevin wanted to find a simple job where he could make a little bit of money, and he ended up working at Fazoli's for a few months. It was a fast-food Italian restaurant. He worked in the dining room area and enjoyed talking with the customers, asking them how their lunch or dinner was, then he would clean up the tables. He thought the girls that worked there were pretty cute too. This one girl would say that she would take out the trash, and Kevin said he would watch her. He really should have walked outside with her to learn how to do it for himself. She thought he was kind of creepy and complained to the manager about him, saying that he wanted to watch her, but honestly, Kevin was just awkward and didn't choose the best words at that moment. The manager had a talk with Kevin, and he felt really bad and embarrassed about it. His state of mind was already fragile, and this situation didn't help. He went into the hospital a short time later with feelings of suicide again and never returned to work at Fazoli's.

Three days before his eighteenth birthday, Kevin told us that he wasn't sleeping well. He said he had been up for three days straight. I know that he dozed a little bit, but he was still obsessed with the online game Gemstone and would play it all hours of the night and then get up and go to school. He only had a few more months of high school, and then he would graduate. We sure hoped he was going to be able to graduate with his class. Every day was a challenge; you never knew what mood he would be in. The online games he played had a profoundly negative effect on his mood and personality.

That same night, we ate dinner at Jack in the Box, and Kevin brought part of his dinner home and put it in the refrigerator for later. We went to bed, but Kevin was still awake, which was quite normal. Around midnight, there was a knock on the door. We heard someone say "Police." *What?* We had been sleeping, and we jumped out of bed and looked over the inside railing and found the police standing in our front entryway. We quickly went downstairs to find out what was going on. Apparently, Kevin decided to gather up his favorite books and coins and leave the house. He was mad at us, but we weren't sure "why" this time we never really were. He was feeling suicidal and had called 911. The police met Kevin outside of our house, and he told them that he was hungry and that we were bad parents and hadn't fed him in over a week. The police officer gave him a granola bar, and he ate it like a little gerbil holding its food and gobbling it down as if we had starved him. We thanked the police for giving him the granola bar, and said that Kevin's leftovers from dinner were in the refrigerator...would you like to see them? Would you like to check our cupboards and refrigerator to see that he had access to ample selections of food? The police said they didn't need to do that. They believed that Kevin was well taken care of and there were other issues going on with him at the time. Since he was feeling suicidal, they needed to take him to the hospital. This time the police drove him there without having to call the fire trucks and ambulances. They felt he was not a danger to himself at that moment and took him to St. Luke's Behavioral Health Center in Phoenix. This time he was there for thirteen days, during which time he turned eighteen.

Now that he was an adult, he wasn't allowed to stay in the children's ward. All the other kids knew that Kevin would be leaving the day that he turned eighteen, so they made him a big poster size birthday card and everyone signed it. It was so kind and thoughtful of them, and we brought in a cake and card and presents. Everyone there sang happy birthday to him and enjoyed some cake; Kevin didn't feel like opening his presents in front of the other kids and said he would open them later. He seemed happy that day, though, not because it was his birthday, but more so because his doctor said to him the day before his eighteenth birthday that she was diagnosing him with Asperger's Syndrome and depression. He felt he had had this for many years, and just never knew what to call it. Now it was confirmed by a doctor, which was incredibly validating for Kevin as well as us, and he felt like someone finally understood him. Kevin was very high functioning, so it wasn't as obvious as some. From a very early age, we had known something was "off," we just never knew what it was.

When the birthday party was over, we walked Kevin downstairs to the adult ward. What a way to spend your eighteenth birthday...

He had been in the adult ward for two days when we got a call from the doctor in charge of his case. The doctor said that Kevin had had some drastic mood changes. He thought he was experiencing a bipolar disorder episode and wanted to do a CT Scan on him. We said yes, to go ahead and do the CT Scan. Later that day we called to check on Kevin, and the doctors moved him to the Level 1 unit for those on suicide watch. Hearing that was beyond disturbing; we weren't sure if he was truly feeling suicidal because it came out of the blue, and I guess we thought he was progressing better than that. After spending one day there, he wanted to go back to the regular ward. He was telling the nurses that he had felt suicidal, but it didn't mean he would try anything and was feeling better now.

Then, Kevin confided in us and told us he didn't like it in the Level 1 unit because there was only a TV. He was bored and wanted back onto the floor where he originally was because there was a ping-pong table, pool table, and other freedoms. He stayed there for a couple of days and then he was moved out to the regular area with everyone else.

During his stay in the hospital, an administrator from Value Options (a coordinated behavioral health care system) came and talked to Kevin. He determined that Kevin needed further evaluation. He explained that he wanted Kevin to be evaluated for SMI (Serious Mental Illness). With this diagnosis, he would be able to receive the right services that he needed to get him well. We agreed that this was a good move in the right direction.

While Kevin was finishing up the last few months of high school, he went to many doctors' appointments, counseling sessions, and was evaluated by a Psychiatrist to see if Kevin was truly SMI. That doctor did consider his situation to be SMI, and after consulting with his counselor, it was suggested that it would be good for Kevin to live in a group home.

That caught us off guard. We had never thought he needed to be away from us. The doctor we met with explained that Kevin would receive more one on one attention and services that we couldn't give him when we were at work. We thought about it, how Kevin was at home and alone most of the time and agreed that it would be good for Kevin to experience living away from us. After all, he was an adult now. The counselor said he would start looking for a group home for Kevin.

He graduated from high school in May 2006 from e-Institute. We were so very proud of him, and we could tell that he was also very proud of himself. There were probably two-hundred students graduating that night, and they all wore blue caps and gowns. It was a great evening watching him walk across the stage and receive his diploma. It was a true achievement for our son that day. His grandparents were also there to watch him graduate, and they were also incredibly proud of Kevin.

Graduation from High School in 2006

Now that he had graduated from high school there would be many hours of doing nothing at home except playing the Gemstone game that he was addicted to. His counselor had been looking for a group home for Kevin and finally, there was one spot available for him. It was in Mesa. There would be planned activities, group and individual counseling sessions, and workshops to prepare for working a job. He would have his own bedroom and share a kitchen and living room area, and there would be three other people that lived there, too. This group home would be staffed twenty-four hours a day, and there were house rules to follow, where they took turns making dinner and cleaning the house and doing their own laundry. We talked to Kevin about it, and he was kind of excited, but mostly scared, which was understandable. He had never been away from us, but we said we would visit him every weekend.

He did end up moving in, but after about six months Kevin wanted to come back home. His social worker said that he wasn't progressing anymore and that the group home wasn't a benefit to him any longer and would be better off living at home instead. Kevin was bored with the same weekly activities they did for the day programs, and he didn't like the food that the others prepared at the house. For most of the six months he lived there, Kevin brought in his own food that he preferred because he was trying to lose some weight and eat healthy, and the menu at the house was either fried or fattening, and he didn't want to gain back the weight he had lost. I'm sure there was more going on at the house that he didn't like, and Kevin would push the staff to let him leave by showing them how unhappy he was there. That in and of itself showed that Kevin was not thriving there any longer. In addition, when he made up his mind about something, he was very persistent to get what he wanted.

Now that Kevin was back home with us and was a legal adult, we felt he needed to be able to get around town and do things so that he wasn't stuck at home like he was previously before going into the group home. A couple of years earlier he was driving our Hyundai Elantra and did very well. We thought it was time that he could handle a car of his own, so we bought him an Isuzu Rodeo. It was a stick shift, very different from the Hyundai which was an automatic. We took him to an open field where he could practice shifting gears, but he was determined to NOT learn how to drive a stick shift. He would not have anything to do with that truck. He liked to sit in it in front of the house in it, but that's all. We threw our money away on that truck and ended up selling it.

Kevin had his bicycle though and went everywhere on that, until one day he thought he wanted a moped. He thought a moped would be easier to ride when it was 110 degrees outside in the Arizona heat. We researched mopeds and found a nice one that was reasonably priced. It could get up to speed (about 45 mph) to keep up with traffic, but not fast enough to be legal on the freeway. Kevin had to take a motorcycle driving test to drive on the road, and he passed it with flying colors. He liked it and went everywhere on it. He promised me that he would always wear his helmet, and as far as I know, he never broke that promise. I'd think that the helmet would be very restricting, but it didn't bother him. Kevin said it was easier to see things on the road and was less distracting. I guess that having processing issues and making quick decisions would be more challenging for someone with Asperger's, and I had heard that some people with Asperger's never learn to drive, so Kevin was ahead of his game. He felt more comfortable on the moped, so that was his mode of transportation. We offered him our car to drive, but he never would. He was a good driver, but he said he was more comfortable on the moped. Everything was going well and fairly normal for what we considered was "normal" in our family life.

*　*　*

Coins and magic were still some of his favorite hobbies, and he felt tormented at times because he couldn't decide which hobby he actually liked the best. One night when Kevin was manic and hadn't slept for a couple of days; he walked to the nearby twenty-four-hour Walmart around 2:00 in the morning. He always had his sponge balls and coins with him wherever he went. There was a McDonalds inside this Walmart, and one of the patrons sitting there enjoying his meal was a guy named Jake. Kevin walked up to this guy and said, "Want to see a magic trick?"

"Sure," Jake said. "I do magic too."

They became instant friends. Kevin had found someone like him, and they had something in common – magic. What are the odds that at 2:00 in the morning on a random night, Kevin would meet someone who was also interested in magic tricks? I'm not entirely sure what both of them were doing in a Walmart in the middle of the night, but it sounded like Kevin was innocently looking for someone to show his magic tricks to. The two of them hung out off and on throughout the next several years. Kevin would help Jake record magic videos and then post them on YouTube. It was nice that Kevin had a friend, even if it was a bit of a sporadic friendship.

He was still interested in coin collecting, but he wasn't obsessed with it; however, he still liked coins. He had a gold piece that was purchased at a reputable store, and since it was evaluated by NGC and PCS as being "the real thing," you would figure you didn't have to worry about it being fake. Well, Kevin did worry. He obsessed over whether it was fake or not. He always thought there was still a chance his coin was fake. So, what did he do? He scratched his beautiful gold coin to see if it was real. He still wasn't convinced. He also posted on the coin forums what he had done to his gold coin. Of course, the other members razzed him good, for many years, over scratching a perfectly good gold coin.

He seriously didn't want to purchase a counterfeit coin and was worried that he would someday, so he attended a two-day class presented by the American Numismatic Association School to learn more about coin conservation and authentication and grading of coins. He wanted to be able to spot a fake and learn more.

On one of the coin forums he belonged to, he met an older gentleman named Dennis who also lived in Surprise. Dennis said he wanted to show Kevin the ropes of how to buy and sell coins on the internet and at coin shows. Dennis wanted to meet with us to discuss how he wanted to help Kevin and it would also help Dennis. He wanted us to know that everything was on the up and up. We invited him to our home and had a very nice visit with him. He had been collecting for many years and would purchase coins from estate sales and had built up quite a collection. Kevin helped him with the advertising and mailing out the sales they made on the internet, and he also had better eyesight than Dennis, so he would photograph the coins for the advertisement. Dennis was very patient with Kevin, which is something he needed.

About once a month, Dennis would pick Kevin up around 6:00 am, and they drove to the coin show in Scottsdale where Kevin would help Dennis sell his coins. Kevin liked shopping at the other vendors' booths, and he usually found something he was interested in purchasing. It gave him a new goal to work toward. They worked together for a year or so, but unfortunately, Kevin wasn't willing to invest his time in learning from him. Dennis tried very hard working with him, but Kevin decided he wanted to spend more time practicing his magic and becoming a performer. His decision to stop working with Dennis tore him up inside. Kevin felt like he was betraying him. Dennis was so hopeful that Kevin would have as much interest in the coin business that he had, but that wasn't the case. Kevin was more interested in perfecting his magic tricks than selling and collecting coins. Performing magic won out, and eventually, Kevin and Dennis went their separate ways.

* * *

One night when Paul was at work, Kevin was yelling and screaming and throwing a fit; He was around nineteen at the time, and I was in the kitchen while he was ranting and raving about how he was upset with his online game or a forum he was a part of. He came into the kitchen and exclaimed "I just sat on one of the rabbits and I think I killed it." I ran into the living room, and there was this poor innocent bunny just lying there. I couldn't believe Kevin would do something so cruel and sad and scary as that. Then he said he did it because he was mad at his dad for giving so much attention to the rabbits and not him. He said that his dad talked to the rabbits in a certain way that made him feel like the rabbits were more special and more important than him. I was really afraid that time. He was acting so erratic that evening and raging about the bunnies and how he hated his life.

I didn't feel safe in the house being alone with him. I quickly grabbed my car keys and purse and got into the car quickly and drove to Paul's work. I told him what had happened, and together we called 911 and asked the police to meet us back at the house.

The police were always very polite and patient with Kevin. They said they had been given special training to handle mental health conditions and understood that sometimes one just needs to talk things through with someone who was having a manic episode. The police knew that sometimes people in a manic episode didn't understand why and what they were doing, and what the consequences could be, so the police would take a little extra time to explain everything to the person and talk them down. I appreciated hearing that because I'm sure that Kevin wasn't the only person who called on them in need of help for similar things. They helped make him understand that he needed to go to the hospital where they could evaluate him and see how they could help him even further. After all of this, Kevin went to St. Luke's Behavioral Health Department again for another visit.

There were many times where Kevin would go into a rage, but he didn't end up going to the hospital. We were able to talk with him and diffuse the situation. One time he took my large Ginsu knife and was pointing it at his stomach and shaking as he was holding it to himself and saying that he wanted to die and that he hated his life. We hid all of the kitchen knives in the house after that happened.

It was difficult to figure out when or what was going to set him off into a rage or a feeling of total despair. It could be something happening in one of his game forums, or magic, or coin forums, or Paul and I asking him to pick up his messy room or empty the dishwasher. The littlest things could set him off, and he was out of control. Occasionally we would wake to find Kevin just standing in our bedroom doorway. We didn't know how long he had been standing there, or why. It was an uncomfortable feeling, and he could never explain to us why he was just standing there. Did he want to talk with us? or was he thinking of doing something bad to us? That was around the time we began locking our bedroom door at night because we weren't feeling safe in our own home.

Years ago, it was suggested that we needed to be nearer the center of Phoenix where there were more social service programs available that might help us with Kevin. We decided to move to Mesa, Arizona during the summer of 2007, where we rented a house to test the waters on the east side of Mesa. We thought that maybe a change of scenery and different social programs would be helpful; at least that's what the social workers were telling us. Kevin was introduced to a new team of social workers and counselors on the far east side of Mesa, where he did find a couple of mentors he liked and spent some of his days just hanging out with them. They must have been discussing working out, losing weight, and dating, because of all of a sudden, Kevin was super motivated to lose more weight, to work out, and eat healthier. He joined a gym that was close to our house, and he even joined an online dating site. He would always jump into something with 100% enthusiasm and the best of intentions. If he was interested, he was completely focused and compelled to go through with it. The online dating site wasn't his best experience, but at least he tried it. No one was interested in dating him through the site, as he didn't have a car or a job, so how would he pick up his date and how would he pay for it? I gave him credit for trying, but we tried to explain to him how maybe his timing was a little bit off just then. He was very disappointed and felt unwanted and unloved. I felt so bad for him, and he said he felt like a failure. It was an awful feeling, and it was hard to watch him experience that.

Along with his positive diet changes, he would bicycle to the gym and work out for a couple of hours a day. He was very determined to lose the rest of the weight that he felt was hanging on. I was so proud of him, and I just watched him in awe. Some people have trouble losing twenty pounds, and then they gain it back again. When he made up his mind to lose weight, nothing stopped him. That's where his Obsessive-Compulsive Disorder (OCD) helped him.

I remember when he was cutting up fresh vegetables in the kitchen. Now that was a different sight from eating mostly fast food. He would order salads without salad dressing. He would order it on the side and would use it sparingly. Kevin would tell me, if you're hungry, eat a bell pepper. He was always saying that. I take his advice to this day when I'm hungry, and I will reach for a red bell pepper. It works! It does fill you up.

All three of us would walk the dogs at night which was good for everyone. Kevin started using the Nintendo Wii to track his exercising. Then he began running. He was so serious and dedicated to losing the weight, and his dad and I were so proud of him for reaching a healthy weight. Sometimes I guess, being focused and obsessive about getting healthy can be a good thing. This was a great time for us to see him harness what was normally a struggle and turn it into something positive.

He ended up losing 105 pounds over a period of three years; being very consistent and by adopting a healthy lifestyle by making better and healthier choices and regular exercise. He was developing a six-pack. His body fat level reduced to 11%. How do we know that? Well, he heard of this test he could take where he floated in water, and they measured how much body fat he had. Of course, he had to do the test. I remember driving him there and waiting for him to complete the test. They gave him a printout, and it showed 11%. He was happy with 11%, but not content. He wanted to go down to 9% body fat. Since he had been so overweight, he had loose skin that covered his six-pack. This bothered him a lot. If you're a person with an obsessive behavior, things can go too far. That's where OCD becomes dangerous. He kept working out at the gym and lifted weights and gained some nice muscles. He was looking very "cut," but it was now going from a healthy harnessing of his struggle and becoming another compulsive disorder.

* * *

One Saturday, we attended the Autism Speaks Walk in Tempe, AZ. There were over 500 walkers and runners that day. Kevin was a part of it too. While his dad and I were filling up our shopping bags with all sorts of healthy granola bars and samples of vitamins the vendors were giving away and speaking with different representatives about autism and learning about the services they were offering. Kevin was in the race, and we all had a great time that day until we noticed that the race was over, and most of the runners had finished. *Where is Kevin?* I asked. We waited and waited for him to show up, and we went looking everywhere that we could think. Finally, we asked one of the security guards for help. He said, "Hop on the security cart and let's find him." He was concerned for Kevin also, mainly because the race had ended and the "water" points that were set up to assist the runners were being taken down. We didn't know where he was or if there was still some bottled water out there for him. One can get dehydrated very quickly in the heat, and it seemed like forever that we were looking for him. Then all of a sudden, we spotted him on the other side of the Tempe Lake. We had been calling him on his phone, but the cell phone service was weak in that area. Finally, we got ahold of him, and we told him to stay put. The security guard drove quickly over the bridge to the other side of the lake where Kevin was. We asked him how he got separated from the other runners, and he said that he was following them, and when he looked up, they were gone, and he was running by himself. He wasn't sure how it happened. I'm just glad that nothing bad had happened that day, and that we all went home safe, albeit very tired.

* * *

Kevin was always researching something. He was fascinated with everything. He loved to read and learn new things. One day he entered a United States typing championship contest where thousands competed. The prize was a special keyboard that could help him type even faster than he already did, and a trip to New York along with recognition as the fastest typist around. He entered the contest and typed around 169 wpm with 98% accuracy. That's lightning speed for most of the world and certainly to me, and he qualified for the semi-finals. He was watching the rankings and saw he was number two or three in the contest. He lost interest at that point because he wasn't the fastest.

A couple of weeks after the contest ended, he looked at his emails, and found out that he had qualified for the finals! The sad part is, he never saw that email in time to respond to it to claim his prize. He felt so bad about it, and it was unfortunate, but I don't think he ever forgot to check his emails from that point on.

TURNING POINT WITH MAGIC

We were still living in Mesa, and Kevin was around nineteen years old when he discovered a magic DVD produced by Ponta the Smith called SICK. It was coin magic. This DVD propelled Kevin into becoming focused on coin magic more than he had been in years past, as well as Ponta's style of performing. He was mesmerized by how good Ponta the Smith was. He wanted to become as good of a magician as he was. That was a turning point in Kevin's love for magic; he became more involved in it and practiced constantly. He was always wanting to show Paul and me a magic trick.

One day, Kevin decided to send a private message to Ponta the Smith through his Illusionist website and asked him how he got to be so good at coin magic. Ponta responded and said that he has put in many hours of practice. Probably about ten-thousand hours on one trick. Ponta was a world-renowned performer who lives in Osaka, Japan, who made a living at performing his magic. Kevin was so very impressed! They began communicating more often via Skype, and Ponta took a liking to Kevin. They had an arrangement where Kevin would help Ponta learn to speak and write English, and Ponta would help Kevin with his Japanese and magic. Ponta had a profound effect on Kevin's mood and motivated him to keep practicing. Kevin always said that Ponta was a true master of coin magic, definitely one of the best coin magicians in the world. There were times when I'd be walking by Kevin's room, and there was Ponta on Skype with Kevin. Ponta would say out loud "Hi Kevin's mom," I'd say "Hi, how are you?" and I'd go on my way. The relationship they had went on for several years.

MOVING TO CHANDLER

Whad been living in far east Mesa for about three years by that point and driving into Chandler for work which was about a half hour away. We decided it was time to move a little closer to my job and nearer to other services for Kevin. First, we were too far west of Phoenix, and now too far east of Phoenix. Mesa had been a little better as far access to social services, but Chandler would be even better. Kevin was still having to travel far to meet with his doctor for regular visits. In 2010, we found a house in Chandler that was more centrally located to Kevin's doctor, and my job, too.

Kevin was assigned a new behavioral health mentor and attended their "day" programs near our new home. His mentor picked him up at the house and would transport him to the programs. In the beginning, we thought these group sessions were great for him. Later on, they became distressing to Kevin and found they hurt more than they helped. He would research what was talked about in the group sessions thinking that maybe he had the same problems that the other people had.

Kevin had been looking forward to the May 2011 IMX (International Magic Experience) All-Star event for about a year, and he signed up for it as soon as the registration opened. There were going to be over thirty accomplished magicians gathering to teach other interested magicians what they knew. They were holding classes to share and teach other magicians the tricks of their trade. His mentor, Ponta the Smith, was going to be there and was also teaching a class. Kevin was so excited to meet him, especially since it would be the first time meeting him in person. They had known each other for almost three years and had Skyped off and on during that time. They told each other that if they ever met, Ponta would bring him some official Poki from Japan, and Kevin promised Ponta a nice silver dollar coin for performing his coin magic. I remember us all driving to Lake Havasu to visit with my dad, Kevin's grandpa, and getting up early the next morning and driving to Las Vegas for the IMX the next morning. Kevin was excited and nervous. We helped him check into his event, and he had a great day. That evening Kevin went to dinner with Ponta and his entire entourage to a Japanese restaurant. Kevin tried some new cuisine and had a great evening with Ponta and some of the other magicians at the conference that day. He really enjoyed himself, and it was a memorable event for all of us.

About a month after having a nice trip to Las Vegas and Kevin spending time with his mentor, Ponta the Smith, Kevin was feeling bad again. Here is part of what he posted on the website www.WrongPlanet.net on June 22, 2011.

I've been diagnosed with Asperger's and major depression...for some reason; I tend to always interpret things people say about me the wrong way, to a negative way, or thinking they don't like me. Events too. Anytime I get praise on something; I just assume it's flattery (i.e., not sincere) or, thank them but discount it later. I have a very hard time accepting compliments. Sometimes I'll just stay up late/early morning reading on the internet in tears...I'm a bit wary of posting here as I've heard some people not getting the right type of feedback. Yes, I've been suicidal, been in the hospital many times, people say sometimes I'm acting this way for attention. I hate that. I just want to prove them wrong sometimes and just kill myself. But I won't do that; I just feel damn trapped.

Looking back on things now, maybe Paul and I should have attended a few of the day programs with Kevin. Maybe we would have learned about something else that would have been of more help to him with his struggles, but we were both working, and Kevin was an adult. We thought that our presence wouldn't have been welcomed.

INDEPENDENCE

Kevin still hadn't lived on his own completely yet, and being twenty-three years old, we thought it would be good for him to live away from his parents to gain some independence. We spoke with his behavioral case worker about it, and he said he would start looking for an apartment that provided some support and stability that was monitored by staff social workers but would enable Kevin to live independently. That sounded good to us. In the meantime, Kevin and Jake were in contact again. Jake was still working part-time jobs and doing magic. They hadn't seen each other since we had moved to Mesa since it was some ways away. Chandler was a little closer, but still a good fifty miles away from Surprise, where Jake lived. When Jake heard that Kevin might be moving out to an apartment, he thought Kevin should get an apartment with him so that they could be roommates. Jake was recently separated from his wife, and they had a baby and needed a new place to live, but what Jake wasn't saying is that he really just needed someone who could qualify for the apartment and wanted to use Kevin for his income and credit. Apparently, Jake had gotten kicked out of a couple of apartments for not paying his rent. At least that's what he had told Kevin in the past.

They started looking for a place to rent, and Paul and I were concerned about the whole situation. What if Jake lost his job and couldn't come up with his share of the rent, then Kevin would be on the hook for all of it, and Kevin lived on a fixed income. What would they do if they didn't have their rent money? Probably call mom and dad. We began steering Kevin away from thinking this was a good idea, and then Jake started bad mouthing us. He told Kevin that we were lying to him and saying we just didn't want him to move out, and wanted to keep him under our control, and who knows what else. Kevin became very angry with us, and we couldn't figure out why. We just knew that he was acting out a lot and talking extra mean to us. Finally, he told us that Jake had been bad mouthing us and saying these lies to him so he would want to get an apartment with him.

We explained to Kevin what we thought Jake was trying to do and the reasons why he needed Kevin to sign the rental contract. He thought about it and realized that Jake was just using him and maybe Jake wasn't the friend he thought he was. He was deeply hurt when this happened and never expected a friend would do that.

Kevin said he didn't know what to believe anymore. Who could he trust? He didn't even feel he could talk to us about some of his issues he was having. He said it's always "his problem." He said, "I see Jake every time I log onto Facebook, and the memories still haunt me in his dreams, both good and bad." He told me, "I don't want to remove him as a friend because I'm a little afraid of him since he's had a shady past. I don't want to associate with him anymore. He was my only friend I ever did anything with, in recent years at least." Kevin was very disturbed by this and was disillusioned by the fact that his friend Jake turned out to not be a true friend.

Not too long after learning that his friend Jake wasn't the person he should rent an apartment with, his case worker found a place for Kevin to move into. It was only a couple miles away from our house and had minimal supervision. Kevin was worried about being able to see us when he moved out on his own and would tell us that he felt like we were abandoning him. I reassured him that we weren't, we simply wanted to help him grow up and find independence so that he could enjoy learning and making his own decisions. I would tell him "You can come over to our house anytime you want to. You'll always have your bedroom here with us." That did make him feel more at ease with moving out on his own.

Shortly before moving into his apartment, he got into an accident on his moped. It was around 8:15 in the morning and the streets were busy with people hurrying to work. He smashed it up pretty good. Another car moved into his lane quickly, and he put his brakes on but swerved so he wouldn't hit the driver in front of him. Other drivers said he did a good job at defensive driving, but there was still a crash. I got a call from Kevin at the hospital and heard him say that he had been in an accident. I started shaking; I couldn't stop thinking that the baby I fought so hard for had been in an accident and was at the hospital. It was a phone call no parent ever wants to hear. I quickly called Paul at his work, and we rushed right over. Kevin was scraped up and bruised a bit, but other than that, he would heal. The police officer said he was glad to see that Kevin had his helmet on, or things could have been much worse.

From that day forward, he never drove his moped again. He learned how to use the city transit system and got a bus pass to get himself to his doctor's appointments and around town. He also rode his bicycle everywhere and went on long rides. Kevin was very resourceful when he wanted to be.

In September of 2011, at the age of twenty-three, Kevin moved into his first apartment. He was independent for the first time, and his dad and I were so happy for him to experience living on his own. He moved into a two-bedroom apartment with a roommate. There were eight apartments in this complex, and everyone who lived there had some disability where they needed a little bit of support to be able to live on their own. Southwest Behavioral Health managed the apartments and monitored the tenants living there independently with minimal supervision. The staff checked on all the tenants several times a day and would take them to their doctor's appointments if needed, and to the grocery store, as well as to fun activities like going to the movies, shopping at the mall, bowling and going to the bookstore. I think Kevin liked the mall the best. He would go straight to the food court and order a Greek Shawarma pita sandwich and Baklava. He also he loved to read, so he bought a lot of books from Bookman's book store.

The rent was low and affordable on Kevin's fixed income. Kevin received Social Security Disability Income (SSDI). This allowed him to pay for his apartment, food, and a few miscellaneous items. He had his own checking account and managed it well, most of the time. Of course, there were times when he wanted something extra, like a new magic DVD or something that didn't fit into his budget, so his dad and I would help him out. We tried different budgeting methods with Kevin when he came up short before the next pay period. First, he would write out the rent check, and then figured he could spend what was left over any way he wanted. That didn't last long because he usually had too much month left before the next payday. What worked best was every week, he would withdraw $80.00 for the week, and he knew that's all he could spend on groceries, eating out, and anything extra like a new book for the week. It was easier to manage seven days at a time, than a full thirty days. When the money was gone, it was gone. We held onto his debit card, and he would have to come to us if he needed more money. Then we could have a discussion about where he had spent it and why it didn't last the seven days and turn the discussion into a learning event.

We would see him quite often after work, and would all eat dinner together, and then he was ready to go back to his place. A couple of times a month he would want to stay over at our house. I would offer for him to bring his laundry with him and he could use our washer and dryer, which saved him a little money since his apartments had coin-operated machines. He also knew that if he started the laundry at our house, most likely mom would end up finishing it. I have to admit; I didn't mind. It would give him a little extra free time to not be stressed out. Most of the time he did his own laundry, he still had his independence and was learning to clean, cook, shop for his food and get to his doctor appointments and day programs on his own.

Living on his own came with some challenges, however, like learning to clean up after himself and keep his room clean as well as the kitchen. Kevin had a tendency to be sloppy, so things got pretty messy at his apartment, and the staff would have to get on his case a little bit to clean it up. His dad and I would go over there and just shake our heads at how messy it was. There is often a misconception that people who live with OCD are always very clean and tidy, and while that may be true in certain cases, it wasn't true for Kevin. Sometimes we helped clean up a little bit or helped to organize his things, but it didn't last long. His roommate ate mostly packaged frozen dinners and occasionally used a plate. When he did use a plate that needed washing, he would do a quick rinse and put it back in the cupboard. It didn't matter if it was clean or not. It was clean to him. They both had their issues and learned to get along with each other most of the time.

Kevin was getting very good at his coin magic and practiced many hours perfecting a trick. He would watch different magic DVD's perfecting his craft. He still kept in contact with Ponta and felt very fortunate to have him as a mentor.

Right around the time he moved into his apartment, Ponta asked Kevin to be a part of a new magic DVD project he and some other magicians were working on. Ponta was producing for Mottsun's DVD called Monster. Mottsun was the performer in the DVD, and they wanted Kevin's voice as the English dub over for the English translation. They needed him to provide the natural English translation from Japanese to English. To do this, Kevin needed to be able to read and speak Japanese. He was so excited to be a part of this project. He felt very honored that his mentor, Ponta, would suggest that he help on it.

Kevin had self-taught himself Japanese over the past year or so. It was a language he loved and was picking it up quickly. Kevin gave Ponta and Mottsun suggestions to correct possible translation errors; he wanted the English translation to be correct in the way we speak English. He did this for Ponta's company called French Drop in Osaka, Japan. When he first started working on the DVD, he would practice his lines in a very monotone way. Then one day, a friend of his, Zady, said she could help him sound better if he would modulate his voice to make it sound more interesting and not sound so monotone. She had taken some acting classes and offered to help him. Kevin and Zady always had a great time hanging out with each other. After practicing Zady's techniques, I noticed it had made a big difference. He was speaking with expression and life in his words, and he sounded great. Kevin was instrumental in conveying the meaning with expression in performing the magic trick. He was very excited and proud to work on this project. The DVD was released worldwide in the summer of 2012. Kevin spent about seven months pouring his soul into being a strong asset and contributor on that project. Kevin's words were "I own that issue and am proud of my hard work."

Kevin and Zady laughing and playing video games.

Kevin had become so obsessed with coin tricks but was extremely good at them too. He held a coin in the palm of his hand for almost a year. Why? To strengthen the muscle in his palm. Eventually, he learned to do what is called a muscle pass. The coin would jump from one palm to the next. It looked cool. He learned a lot of different coin tricks and would upload his performances on YouTube for others to see and critique his work. He also joined a couple of magic forums where he posted his routines. It was a place where other magicians could get feedback on their techniques so they could improve. It was mostly constructive, but there were a few other magicians who were not so nice to Kevin, and he would take their comments so personally and couldn't get the bad comments out of his mind. He would obsess over their comments, and it would make him feel depressed, and sometimes this led him down the path of suicidal thoughts again.

Kevin managed pretty well at his apartment for the first four months, but then he went back to St. Luke's Behavioral Health Hospital again for about a week. This time he was feeling suicidal because he would be losing one of his favorite counselors; one that was transferred out to another facility. When you confide in someone and develop a connection with that person, it can be devastating when that person leaves. He had gone through this a couple of times previously, but this time affected him more seriously and all Kevin could think of was dying. It's hard to not get attached to someone, and he needed some time to sort through his thoughts and try to get over his intense sadness of losing a counselor he really connected with. He was assigned a new counselor, and everything was o.k. again.

Kevin was always out and about in the neighborhood riding his bicycle, attending a day class or going to a doctor's appointment. He had lots of energy, and I think he was searching for something new to do. He always had an interest in the martial arts and started with Karate when he was just six years old and moved onto Taekwondo afterward. He was involved in the art, off and on throughout the years. Kevin was so flexible that when he was much younger, he could do the center splits very easily and sit in a "split" position between two chairs while swinging his nun chucks, and although I was his mom and may have been biased, I was still impressed. He was always advancing belts and getting ready to take another belt test. By the time he was twelve years old, he was already a brown belt.

His day group would occasionally go to the movie theater in Tempe, and on one of those day trips, he discovered an Aikido studio right next door around May of 2012. I had never heard of Aikido before. Kevin explained that it was sort of a cross between disciplined Karate and street fighting to know how to get yourself out of a jam if you were on the ground. He observed the class for a couple of weeks before deciding to sign up to learn Aikido. His instructor talked with him a lot and seemed to be very patient with him, which is what Kevin needed, in order to learn. His Aikido classes were twice a week, and he really enjoyed them.

A month later he decided to take an English writing class at Mesa Community College. We thought it was a great idea. He hadn't been in school since graduating high school in 2006, but he felt ready to try out college. His first college class was in June 2012. It was a night class, and the buses weren't running by the time his class was over, so most of the time we would pick him up from class and take him to his apartment afterward.

He enjoyed his first class on writing Rhetoric, although he was much too hard on himself. He would spend so much time working on his assignments and then didn't feel they were good enough and was having a difficult time dealing with school and life in general again. We were worried that it was just too much for him at the time. He was still taking his Aikido class a couple of times a week, along with the English writing class twice a week. He did manage to complete his summer class, and we were very proud of him for taking on that huge responsibility.

It was a difficult schedule going to go college part-time and continuing with his Aikido class. That doesn't sound like much for some people, but he had to arrange his transportation to doctor's appointments or ride his bicycle or take the city bus, not to mention the mental exhaustion of his processing issues and other mental health struggles. It was a lot to juggle. I always thought he did a great job figuring out the bus schedule and planning his trips, so he arrived on time.

Kevin was curious and inquisitive about everything. He asked a lot of questions, and read countless books from many genres and subjects, including sociology, psychology, economy, chemistry, philosophy, numismatics, and taught himself Japanese for one to two years before he took an actual Japanese course.

A month later, in August of 2012, his psychiatrist told Kevin he thought he had a "personality disorder." In Kevin's case, this meant that he had a rigid and unhealthy pattern of thinking and behaving no matter what the situation. He was told that it can lead to significant problems and limitations in relationships, social encounters, work and school. Now Kevin has something new to research on the internet and find out if the doctor was correct. Kevin was also told that he might have Body Dysmorphic Disorder (BDD) because he was very obsessed with his body image still and wanted a low Body Mass Index (BMI). He focused so much on these things that it interfered with his happiness and ability to function. He was determined to have a doctor diagnose him with Body Dysmorphic Disorder (BDD), so he could go to a clinic where he could get help. We discovered later that he had struggled with bulimia and was a contributing factor to him losing so much weight. This is something he hid from us for a very long time.

The day group Kevin attended arranged a camping trip in the mountains the next month. He was so excited to go on this trip, and we were excited for him too. The first night there, he spilled soda on his box of pills, so he went to the bathroom to wash off the sticky soda. Some water got into the pill box and dissolved his medication. Kevin understood that he needed this medication and without it, he could become unbalanced and feel very bad. He became very anxious and depressed and was obsessing over the fact that he didn't have his medication. The staff wasn't able to calm him down, so they called an ambulance to pick him up and take him to the local hospital. They said they couldn't take him themselves because they had to stay with the others. Since the staff knew of Kevin's past for severe recurrent depression and suicidal ideation, they didn't feel he should stay at the camp since he would be off his medications for that short trip. It was really unfortunate this happened because he was so looking forward to the entire trip.

The staff called us the next day and asked us to pick him up from the hospital. He was at Pine View Hospital in Lakeside, Arizona which was in the White Mountains and over two hours away. Their doctor evaluated Kevin and gave him his regular meds. During this evaluation, Kevin was so insistent that he had an eating disorder and wanted to be treated at a hospital that could help him get through this problem; he convinced the doctor of his problem. The doctor agreed and wrote all about it in his discharge instructions of what his new diagnosis was at that time. Kevin was happy to know that someone, finally, believed him; that he had an eating disorder. It was another feeling of validation for Kevin.

It took us two hours to reach Kevin and check him out of the hospital, only to drive back seven hours into Morongo Valley, California. That same day, my brother called me and said that our Mom was in the hospital and having emergency surgery, so then we drove out to be with her. It was a very long day. When it rains, it pours. Life calmed down for my mom after the surgery, and she was finally feeling well, but then Kevin was in crisis again.

About a month later, Kevin went to Aurora Behavioral Health Hospital. He was stressed, depressed and was having suicidal ideations. The timing of his episodes to a behavioral hospital was becoming more frequent and severe in Kevin's reaction to his situation. The frequency and severity were really worrying us. Hearing this again and again left me drained, worried beyond belief, and numb. It's hard getting those phone calls because you fear the worst, hope for the best, and never know how serious each crisis is going to be. It was exhausting. His dad said to me one day, "You know that he really might just kill himself one of these days." I said I knew that, and feared it, but we agreed that we had to keep trying to get him the help he needed and just be there for him. It was like walking on eggshells, even when we were asleep.

This behavioral health facility was like Fort Knox. We had never been to a hospital where the security was so tight and had so many rules. When we went to visit him, we had to lock our keys and any personal belongings in a locker and then give the locker key back to the receptionist. Then a group of us were escorted into a large room for visiting hours during specified hours only.

He was there for three weeks, during which time he attempted to strangle himself with his T-shirt. Thank goodness, he was unsuccessful, but they sent him to another hospital to x-ray his throat to see if he hurt anything in his neck. Thankfully nothing had been damaged. In previous times of distress, Kevin hurt himself when he was alone, or he acted out, and his actions sent him to the hospital. This time he acted out in a more severe and distressful way and did it while he was still in the hospital. That was more disturbing to me because it showed a more elevated sign of acting out on a suicide attempt. He spent twenty-one days there, the maximum time allowed to stay under his insurance plan. I kept thinking to myself over and over, *when will Kevin catch a break? When will something good happen for him?*

When it was time to release him, the hospital didn't even bother to call me or arrange for transportation home. Instead, they gave him a bus pass and said: "good luck to you out there." That really bothered me. My initial thought was that it was a horrible thing to do to someone who had been through some very difficult weeks and was in a fragile state of mind. I know those places can be so busy at times though, with few people trying to help so many patients, and sometimes the staff just does the same thing for all discharged patients without the ability to come up with a specific discharge plan for each person. However, if I had known they were going to discharge him that way, I would have left work and picked him up. After seeing things like this happen as many times as I have, I firmly believe that there have to be some changes in our behavioral health care system.

LONELINESS

Kevin wanted to meet new people and was told that socializing could help. That was a really hard thing for him to do, but he decided to do his magic at a local bar. He felt that since magic brightened up his day, it would do the same for others too. He tried several bars and restaurants and was kicked out of most of them. He thought the reason was either "I suck," or "No one gives a crap." He felt he could be himself by showing them a magic trick and share the happiness it brought to him, and it was disappointing to find that wasn't always the case. It sounds good; however, Kevin was under the impression that he could just walk into a restaurant and approach people having their dinner and ask if they wanted to see a magic trick. We tried to explain that doing a magic trick in the restaurant wasn't wrong, but his approach wasn't appropriate. He needed permission from the restaurant first.

Eventually, he did perform magic at Applebee's with permission from the manager, and it was a great evening for him, and we were very proud to see him in action also. He only did this one night, and the restaurant changed their policy and decided to bring in clowns instead who would create balloon figures for the kids.

I found a note in Kevin's room about doing his magic in restaurants:

Is this feeling for importance, this hunger for approval, to "fit in" to feel "appreciated" driving me insane? I mean, I just wanted to do magic to feel appreciated. That's it! I never fit in. I couldn't even do that. And when I explained it to my parents that I tried to go into restaurants and do magic, of course, I was wrong! I didn't know that wasn't OK to do. And I still don't see why the hell not. Am I not good enough at it? Do I just plain suck?

We give him a lot of credit for putting himself out there and trying to socialize and share something that he was so passionate about. It's unfortunate that his intentions weren't received better.

Kevin and I got along pretty well. We were always able to talk about most everything. There were days when we would have some very nice mother and son talks. He would especially want me to sit with him when he was feeling bad. He didn't want me multitasking by doing the dishes or something else; he simply wanted me to just sit there and listen without any distractions. I would listen and try to help him understand his feelings and help him find a solution.

Some of these talks occurred after I found a troubling note he had written; a note just laying on top of his desk for anyone to see. Other times, when straightening his room, I would see the many messy piles of papers where he had written his thoughts that day. There were many notes throughout the years, and it's not that he was trying to hide these notes from Paul or I, they were just there. He never expressed the thought that we were invading his privacy, and because we were so worried about his mental health, we had to be more diligent about watching for warning signs, like notes he wrote talking about wanting to die.

He welcomed me sitting with him in his room and helping him straighten it up. It was the only way anything ever got accomplished. I'd pick something up, and he would say "It's trash," or "Keep it." Then I'd give him a suggestion on where to put it away if it was an item to keep, and he would put it away in its place.

I'm glad we could talk with each other. If not, I think Paul and I would find it easy to believe that Kevin was just a very angry person. Yes, he was angry a great deal of the time, but we could usually talk things out and most of the time bring him out of his feeling of despair to function another day.

It felt as if everything with Kevin's desperate state of mind was escalating. I'm not sure of the exact date, but I do know that Kevin was spiraling down again when I found this note in his room:

"I am sick of living. If I had a gun right now in my hand, it would be over."

He planned to buy a gun from a store up the street from our house and was researching guns and bullets on the internet. He said he wanted people to feel sorry when he died. He has so much pain and angst. He said he wanted to forgive others and himself but didn't know how.

When Paul and I saw the information, Kevin had on his computer screen, we were terrified! At that moment, we didn't know exactly where Kevin was. Did he have a doctor's appointment, was he attending a day class? We couldn't find him anywhere, so Paul and I went to the local gun store, the one that was on his computer showing its location. We took Kevin's old driver's license with us to the gun store and asked them if Kevin had been there and purchased anything from them. The man working there told us that no, he hadn't. That was a relief. We told them not to sell a gun to him; he was not mentally stable and was researching online the best way to kill himself. They took a copy of his driver's license and said they would hang it up on their wall and tell all of their employees NOT to sell to him. Then we went to the Chandler police station to see if they might know where he was. "Maybe they had a report on him?" Paul and I thought to one another. They didn't. We went to Kevin's bank and withdrew all of his money from his account so he wouldn't have access to it to purchase a gun. We were relieved to find that he hadn't drained his bank account. Later on, that day, we found that Kevin had gone to one of his day programs and he was safe, for now.

Another note:

"I hate my dad. I really do. And the hate is just getting worse. It's not getting better. I wrote down the list of stuff I did wrong. NOT ONE positive thing I've heard, in what, half a year or more?"

There were times when Kevin misinterpreted situations as Paul not thinking Kevin could do anything correctly. Paul was trying to teach his son. For instance, walking into a restaurant and doing a magic trick while the customer was enjoying their dinner. A more appropriate place to do that might be in Las Vegas, or at a Chuck E. Cheese restaurant; locking up your bicycle properly that was secure so it wouldn't be stolen. Kevin lost his wallet and cell phone a couple of times. Paul suggested a new wallet with a chain on it, and a holster for the cell phone. Kevin thought his dad was calling him stupid, but he wasn't. He was trying to teach Kevin a better way of doing something. Paul said that he got so frustrated with Kevin because he wouldn't think things out and would made bad decisions. But Kevin interpreted it as being critical and not loving him. Paul said when he was thinking back on their relationship, he realized that he thought that Kevin appeared to others as being "normal" and that Kevin should be able to do anything that was normal and reasonable.

But Kevin wasn't normal in the sense of being able to make the best decision at times. Kevin's thought process was different, and Paul didn't have the patience to deal with him, and it frustrated him.

Another note:

(He was upset that the girl he tried to get in touch with, from a dating site, didn't want to get together with him because he didn't have a job; she never called him.) *"That's okay; it just confirms how worthless I am." Logically, I know this is not true, all of this. But, on the other hand, I feel it IS true. I do FEEL worthless. I don't know how I can even keep my sanity right now.*

Another note:

I don't even feel comfortable talking to them. Now I wrote this; maybe it will be more comfortable to kill myself now. What should I do? I need something that will be a sure-fire way. Something like a bullet to the back of the head.

I don't want to end up paralyzed or mentally challenged in a wheelchair. I just want this to end. The pain, the suffering, I just want a goddamn friend. I can't even make one.

I'm that pathetic I guess. Yeah, I guess I am doing this for attention. I am a coward. Like the guy last time on the phone who said to me on the suicide hotline, "You're suicidal but don't feel you're going to follow through with it? So, you're not suicidal?" Yeah, that's right buddy. I'm not suicidal. We'll see.

Kevin was hurting so badly and for so long. We were at a loss of what to do. We were so afraid that he would commit suicide one day. We had tried so many different things to help him. We tried to be good parents and give him the love and support he needed, and still nothing seemed to be working.

Life really did feel like a roller coaster with Kevin. We never knew what his mood would be from day to day. Everything could be going well, and something said that didn't agree with him could set him into an angry rage, or spiral him into a mode of depression, or worse. It felt like we were walking on eggshells trying to keep his mood even-keeled. I can't imagine how bad he felt inside living on this roller coaster in his mind.

In December 2012, Kevin had been practicing Aikido for about seven months, becoming stronger every week, and was hoping to test soon to earn his yellow belt. It would be his second belt in Aikido and is somewhat akin to getting your third or fourth belt in the other martial arts like Taekwondo and Karate. There weren't as many belts in Aikido.

One night at his class he fell wrong and separated his shoulder. He heard this loud "pop" and was laying on the floor. He was looking forward to testing for the next belt, and now it looked like he would have to put off that goal for awhile. One of the other student's drove him to Chandler Regional Hospital where they treated Kevin, and we rushed over to see him. We picked him up from the hospital after he was checked out and took him home with us for a few days. He was in a lot of pain with his separated shoulder and the swelling and the large deformed bump. It would be a couple of months before this type of an injury healed. His test for his yellow belt would have to wait.

After two months, his injury had finally healed, and he was ready to jump back into Aikido, return to class, and test for his yellow belt. He did very well, and the Sensei video recorded his test. I was so impressed watching Kevin lead the class as part of the testing process. He started out with the warm-up routines, and everyone followed him. It's as if he had been leading the class for a long time. Then he had several testing requirements to achieve, and he passed them all and got his yellow belt. We were so proud of him, and he was proud of himself which was so encouraging to see. He did great! Afterward, his Sensei and classmates went to a local restaurant to have snacks and drink and celebrate Kevin's night. It was a great night!

Aikido Exam March 2013

TOUGH TIMES

In January of 2013, the spring session of college was starting up, and Kevin wanted to take an Algebra and a Japanese class. He has always been interested in writing and speaking Japanese and has a pretty good handle on it so far, but he wanted more. We tried talking him into taking only one of the two classes, because he was still attending his Aikido training twice a week, but he insisted on taking both classes. He had his mind made up, and that was that.

Kevin had been in his Spring classes for only a couple of weeks and had missed some critical attendance days and was dropped from the classes. He was devastated, and the stress of his busy schedule was catching up with him. His classes were three half days of Algebra and two half days of Japanese. He wasn't coping with the schedule of getting there daily and having a lot of homework to complete.

During all this time, he was still obsessing over his weight and his loose skin from losing a hundred and five pounds over the previous three years. He was going the other direction from anorexia to bulimia. We didn't know how bad his eating disorder was affecting him, he seemed to hide it so well. What we saw were the usual depression and rage outbursts, and once in a while he would say that his stomach was upset, and he threw up a little bit, but I never heard him throwing up, and he later told us that he did this when he was around us at home. I guess I just didn't notice what was going on with him in regards to his eating disorder, but I wish I had. Kevin went to the hospital because his stomach hurt a lot, and the doctor checked his gallbladder and first said he might have to have it removed. His stomach was so tender, and his throat hurt a lot and had a lot of indigestion. Looking back on things, this was probably from the throwing up. He wanted his psychiatrist to believe that he had an eating disorder, but his doctor dismissed it as Kevin just being compulsive over it and said that he was fine. Kevin was very upset that his doctor didn't agree with how he was feeling, and decided he wanted to change doctors and go back to the previous one whom he felt he related with better. I know it was hard for him being repeatedly told one thing or another, and not having his feelings validated by those whom he confided in, who he needed the most help from.

On January 13, 2013, Kevin was feeling suicidal again. This time he overdosed on his medications and drank alcohol at his apartment. It was the first time that he added in alcohol, at least that we were aware of, and we were so thankful that he called 911 for help before it was too late. The ambulance took him to Chandler Regional Medical Center as an inpatient for overdosing. We found out about it the next day when the staff from his apartment called us and said he was in the hospital yet again. It's upsetting that the hospital didn't notify us right away, but they didn't. There are the HIPPA laws that don't allow them to unless the patient gives permission. After all, he was an adult and was almost twenty-five years old.

Years later, when I was going through Kevin's papers, I came upon this hospital report. I didn't know until then - the extent of this particular hospital visit.

The hospital report said that "Upon arrival, Kevin stated that he drank a bottle of Saki and took Luvox, an SSRI; Clonazepam, a long-acting benzodiazepine, and Lisinopril, an antihypertensive, around 3:00 am. Poison control said the pills that he took were long-acting, and he might need to be observed for a full 24 hours until no longer somnolent (sleepy, drowsy)."

> His discharge diagnoses:
> 1. Multi-substance drug overdose with suicidal ideation
> 2. Known case of bulimia nervosa
> 3. History of fibromyalgia
> 4. Known case of Asperger syndrome
> 5. Known case of anxiety disorder
> 6. Alcohol intoxication

They kept Kevin there for almost two days at Chandler Regional Hospital, stabilizing him, and then he was transferred to Aurora Behavioral Health Hospital where he spent another nine days. I think this was his third trip to Aurora. He was kept on suicide watch while he was there, which meant his room was in a direct line of sight with the nurses' station so they could see him at all times.

Kevin was just too smart for his own good. He figured out that the staff came by his room every fifteen to twenty minutes. He waited until they came by, and then he attempted to strangle himself with his bedsheet. This time was worse than the previous attempt in the hospital. The nurse entered his room on her next round and found him passed out on the floor, and she yelled "code blue" – bring the crash cart. They were able to bring him conscious and save him, but this was a much closer call. All of this happened in the daytime while we were at work. The hospital called me, and I was so upset to hear this over the telephone, I couldn't think straight, I didn't know what to do; it didn't seem real that this was happening to him. I felt sick to my stomach, upset, and angry with the hospital, all at the same time. With all of their security and having him in their line of sight, you would think that this wouldn't happen to any patient. I was in total shock. I thought they were watching him better; it was beyond scary, especially as he didn't seem to be stable for very long before another event would happen.

Kevin's access to prescription drugs was much too easy. He would meet with his psychiatrist and discuss what was happening in his life at the time. The psychiatrist would sometimes adjust his medication to a different dosage or a different type, and a brand-new prescription was filled by the pharmacy. Sounds like a normal process, but the underlying concern was Kevin already had many unfinished prescriptions in his possession, and that part of the equation wasn't ever monitored by the doctor, apartment staff, or his case worker. He always had his old prescriptions in his possession.

These prescriptions could do a lot of damage if he were to overdose on them which is what happened, but thankfully it wasn't fatal. His dad and I were always concerned by the fact that he had all of these other medications on hand. One day Paul and I contacted his case worker and told him we wanted to remove the extra bottles of prescription drugs that were in his top dresser drawer. He agreed that it was a good idea, and he allowed us to take them from his apartment. After all, this attempted strangulation event happened right after his overdosing, and he was still in the hospital for treatment.

There is a serious disconnect in this area of prescribed drugs, and I wish the behavioral health system would monitor it better. We took Kevin's prescriptions home with us and laid them out on our kitchen stovetop. To our surprise and total disgust, he had enough prescriptions to fill the entire stove top. I counted the pills out and found there were over one-thousand of them at his disposal. It was enough for several people to overdose on. Over the years, Kevin was prescribed many different medications such as Zoloft, Celexa, Paxil, Risperdal, Tenex, Seroquel, Lithobid, Haldol, Tegretol, Geodon, Depakote, Lamictal, Saphris, Neurontin, Trileptal, Vistaril, and Luvox.

Medication can be used in wonderful ways when it is monitored, but the amount Kevin had was not a useful tool, nor was it healthy for him mentally. It was dangerous, it was a problem, and this is not the only example of someone living in America with ready access to things like this. Something needs to change. Behavioral health should be about health, not simply marketing poorly monitored pharmaceuticals.

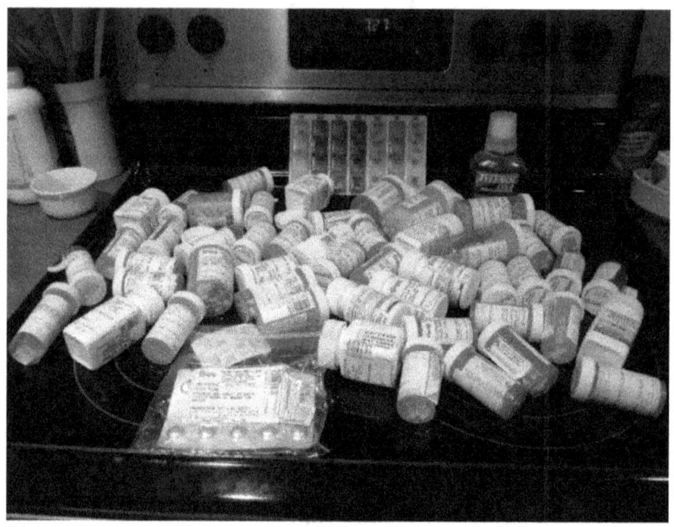

Kevin's prescription medication

The staff who monitored the apartments where he lived was having problems with Kevin cooperating when the staff did their nightly check on all the residents. They began saying that he needed a higher level of care and that he was too high of a risk for the level of care they could provide him with. They told us that they would begin looking for another place for Kevin to live. It did appear that way, and we knew they were right. They also said that if Kevin didn't agree to this arrangement, they could petition Kevin as a danger to himself and get a court order to have him live elsewhere. Paul and I were sure that Kevin would agree to move after explaining it to him, and yes, he did agree. No one had to petition the court. It was decided that it was best for everyone if Kevin found another place to live.

About two weeks after leaving the hospital, they found him a house that was staffed 24/7 and was near the college he attended. That would be good for him, and the new staff offered to drive him to school as well. He liked that. Kevin moved into the new house, and things started out well but changed within a couple of weeks. They added a third roommate, and Kevin knew he was going to have to share the bedroom, but they also asked him to switch bathrooms. The inconvenience of things that might seem small to some people were a big deal to him. It doesn't mean they weren't a big deal, but his ability to process certain things would make issues that might be minor to others a major issue for him. It was a big deal to Kevin that he had to enter the other roommates master bedroom to use their joint bathroom while passing by his roommate if he was sleeping. In addition, there was a wiring problem in the bathroom, and they had no lights. He had to shower and get ready for school at 5 o'clock in the morning in the dark. The food menu there was also very different from Kevin's healthy way of eating, and they couldn't accommodate what he ate, so he was to provide his own food, which became an added expense for him. The straw that really broke the camel's back was that the rent doubled from what they had originally told him it would be. The living arrangement wasn't working out, and that's when Kevin moved back in with us.

I remember calling Kevin while I was at work and told him to start packing up his belongings; his dad and I would be there after work to pick him up and all of his things. He was afraid that the staff wouldn't let him leave. That didn't make any sense to me, but he was feeling very uneasy. It turns out that everything went smoothly, and we drove Kevin home to our house. The other place just wasn't the best living arrangement for him.

OBSESSIVE COMPULSIVE DISORDER IS A SERIOUS MATTER

Paul and I were excited to have Kevin live with us again. It had been about a year and a half since he moved out of our house and into his apartment. His caseworker was looking for another place for him to live, but for now, it felt right for him to be at home with us. He had the opportunity to learn independence and live away from Paul and I, and I think he needed to regroup and relax a little. When he felt ready again, he could find another independent living place, if that's what he decided to do.

Kevin was still taking Japanese and Algebra at Mesa Community College and going to his Aikido class two times a week. Some days were very long. He woke up around 4:00 am to get ready and walk to the bus stop which was about a half mile away. He did this for a few days, but we could see that it was too much to manage and the next week Paul and I started driving him to school and then went on to our jobs.

Since all three of us hadn't spent as much time with each other, it was nice being together again. Still, Kevin's mood swings continued. They went from being very intense and angry over his homework assignments that he had so much work to do; he would suddenly become happy when he finished a homework assignment, or he would take a break and show us a magic trick. Most evenings, Kevin would play video games in his room. Sometimes we would all start out by watching a movie in the living room together, but Kevin lost interest quickly and went to his own room. He wasn't ever big on watching TV. On the weekends we would go out to the movie theater. Kevin knew that would entail getting out of the house and going out to eat. We all enjoyed that. The movies meant popcorn and a drink. We all had a good time at the movies.

Paul and Kevin were getting along well, and they started playing a video game together. They used to always play video games together when Kevin was much younger, and it was a nice way for them to reconnect as adults. After school, Kevin would take the city bus home and start on his homework before we were home from work. This went on for about six weeks.

Kevin was sitting in the circle of those attending a group meeting he had one day, and he noticed the prettiest girl he had ever seen. He gazed at her from across the circle, and I think he fell in love at that very moment. They talked afterward and discovered that they had a lot in common. Over the next few weeks, they got to know one another better and went for pizza one night. It wasn't a date, although Kevin wished it was. She had a boyfriend whom she was having trouble with, and Kevin was hoping they would break up. He didn't think this guy was good enough for her. They also talked about their eating disorders that they both struggled with. She was doing pretty well with her recovery and told Kevin she couldn't hang out with him because when he talks about his issues, it triggered her and her eating disorder. He was so upset when she told him that she couldn't spend time with him anymore because of this; she needed to put her health first, which was so important. All he wanted was a friend, and possibly a girlfriend. I can understand that she needed to be strong to keep up with her commitment to herself to recover, and that's a hard thing to do. I felt so bad for him. It was another sad event he had to live with. He was upset and cried when he told me about what had happened. He said, "I just want someone to love."

On February 13, 2013, Kevin turned twenty-five. We asked him where he wanted to eat dinner to celebrate. He said Tofu-BBQ. It was a Korean restaurant that he liked. I had eaten there once before when Kevin and I ate lunch together one day, and it was alright, just not my favorite type of food. Kevin knew he would get a reaction from his dad to have to eat at a Tofu-BBQ restaurant. It didn't sound good to Paul, but that's what Kevin wanted, so off to the restaurant we went. Kevin got a good laugh out of it, seeing his dad sweating over what on earth was he going to eat. His dad didn't like change, but Kevin was always thrilled to experiment with anything that was different and exciting. I loved that about him. Kevin ordered for all of us that evening, and it wasn't too bad, and Paul survived dinner. Now when we drive by the restaurant, we laugh and think about that last birthday dinner together. It created a nice memory.

In March the following month, Kevin went back to see his original psychiatrist, the one he had just before he moved into his last apartment over a year and a half ago. It was the doctor that he liked and felt understood him the best. Paul and I always thought that Kevin liked him because Kevin could get more of what he wanted from this psychiatrist. Kevin thought he could convince Dr. Neufeld that he really did have an eating disorder and needed to be sent to a facility that treated his problem and believed that only then could he get onto the right track of being healthy. Although he had been diagnosed with bulimia nervosa in the hospital, it never ended up as part of his treatment plan. Kevin needed someone who would finally believe him and see that he had a problem, that he wanted and needed help. I don't know what they discussed in those last sessions, but the doctor changed his medicine, and it didn't agree with him at all. He became very angry and lethargic. He was very difficult to get to school, and he ended up missing a few classes.

A short time later, Kevin got sick with a sore throat and an ear-ache, so his dad took him to his family doctor. She knew Kevin pretty well, and she took one look at him and said, "What is going on with Kevin? What medicine is he on?" He didn't look or sound good, and his doctor was very concerned. We were also worried, and I remember calling his psychiatrist's office the next day. I gave the case manager the information on what his family doctor said and told the office that I didn't think he was on the right medication. They relayed the message, and the doctor made only a slight change. It wasn't enough. Something more needed to be done, but it never happened. He said Kevin would have to set an appointment with him again to make more changes in his medication. Kevin agreed and said he would make an appointment, but he never made it to another appointment with the doctor. It was too little, too late.

Only a couple of days later, on April 12th, 2013 of that same year, Kevin was having a rough day after school. He already wasn't doing well on his medicine, and he was feeling sick, and now he was yelling and very angry and couldn't get his computer at home to work. I remember when he called me at work to tell me this. He could barely contain his frustration and anger. I told him that his dad and I would be home in less than two hours and his dad would fix it. Paul was great at fixing anything, and since he was an IT Data Center Specialist, anything involving computers was his specialty.

As soon as we walked in the door from work, Kevin started yelling at us and throwing a fit. He was overly upset at the fact that he couldn't get onto the computer. Paul was angered by the fact that Kevin was acting out so belligerently; so rudely to us. Paul said, "forget about fixing the computer; you can't talk to us that way." Kevin just didn't understand that he couldn't attack someone just coming in the door and then demand something. That's what a rational person understands; however, Kevin wasn't in a rational state of mind at all. Paul was very angry with him at that moment and just ignored him until after dinner. Kevin was becoming angrier with every passing minute. He was obsessing over the fact that he might not be able to get on the computer that night. It was too much for him to handle. He was on stress overload.

The real story is that Paul just needed to eat some dinner, calm down from being mad at Kevin for being so angry. Paul had every intention of fixing the computer that evening, and he figured out quickly that the problem was the routers power supply failed. He looked everywhere for one and couldn't find an extra one. Kevin was really losing control by this point and was beyond the point of using any of the coping tools he had been taught to use when he felt this way.

He was getting anxious that we weren't going to do anything about it, even though we tried to reassure him that we would go to the store and buy another power supply if we couldn't find one at home. We just needed a few minutes after dinner to look for one. Finally, I went into the garage and looked in the filing cabinet where we kept extra computer supplies. There it was, an old power supply that would work for the router. And it did work! Kevin could now get onto the computer. He quickly calmed down, and things seemed to be semi-normal for the rest of the evening. Kevin felt back in control of being able to get back onto the computer and do what he wanted to do. It didn't take much to set him off into a rage, or an out of proportion response to an event. Handling stress was never something he was able to do.

It had been a very tiring week for me at work, and I was ready for bed around 9:30 p.m. that evening, which was early for a Friday night. Kevin was sitting at the kitchen table writing on the computer. Everything seemed to be back to a normal state for our household. He asked me, "Are you going to bed for the night?" "Yes," I said, "I'm really tired from my week at work. I love you." He said, "I love you too, Mom." Those were the last words we had with each other. Paul and I went to sleep.

About 10:20 p.m. we heard a loud knock at the door. We woke up and said, "Oh no, here we go again." It wasn't the first time the police had knocked on our door in the middle of the night. There were two police officers standing in the doorway. They asked if we knew where Kevin was. We said, yes, he's sleeping in his bedroom. They said they received a call from someone named Kelcey, and that Kevin had posted on Facebook that he was going to kill himself. I immediately asked them to come in, and we went straight to Kevin's bedroom. His door was locked. I looked for the little universal bedroom door key you put in the lock to open it. I couldn't find one, even though we usually kept them over the door frame. Paul said he would get something to open it and headed for the garage.

Shortly thereafter, Paul came back from the garage with a skinny screwdriver, but I had already found the universal key and opened the door. The police and I entered Kevin's room, but Kevin wasn't there. We looked in the closet, and I looked under the bed. He wasn't in his room. That struck me as weird. Where on earth was he? Paul said he would go look to see if he was in the van in the garage. Paul looked in the van and didn't see Kevin and headed back inside the house. Right as the police and I were headed toward the garage, Paul was coming back inside; his back toward the garage door. At that moment, the police officer and I looked past where Paul was standing. We saw Kevin hanging from the ceiling behind our Dodge Caravan. You could see only the very top of his torso. I gasped, and Paul knew right away that it was bad. "What?" he said. I answered, "Kevin is in the garage." Paul turned around and saw him too. Immediately, Paul and the police officer ran to where Kevin was hanging. There wasn't much room on the side of the van to reach Kevin, so the police officer went through the side van door, and the officer used his knife to cut him down. He thought he heard Kevin gasp a little, maybe. Kevin's face was ghost white and had turned half blue. They got him down, and Paul dragged Kevin by his feet away from the side of the van just outside of the garage door opening. Another policeman just stood there looking at Kevin. I said, to the police officer, "Shouldn't you be doing something like pressing on his chest and doing CPR?" I started motioning to do compressions, and the officer then started doing the compressions until the fire department arrived. I almost jumped in there and started compressions myself, but I wasn't sure I should since the police were right there near his head, and I'm not sure that even if I tried the compressions, that I would have pressed hard enough to do any good. I was his mom and was extremely upset and in shock. I'm glad the officer did step in finally. Maybe the officer had never seen anything like this, or maybe he thought that Kevin was a lost cause. I think they should have reacted faster and more automatically, and at the same time when you are in a daze while you watch these things happen...maybe they seem to be going slower than they really are.

The police were asking us questions while the fire department was working on Kevin. I kept looking over to where Kevin was lying and looking to see if he was moving yet.

I asked, "Is he ok?" He wasn't.

The police were trying to distract us by asking questions and taking their report. I knew this and wanted to just stand near Kevin and watch what was going on. I just wanted him to breathe.

Breathe Kevin.

Please breathe.

Breathe. Breathe!

Paul was so surprised that he didn't notice Kevin when he first entered the garage to get a screwdriver to unlock his bedroom door with. He had been so focused on getting something to open up the door with that when he entered the garage a second time he still didn't see Kevin since he was hard to notice behind the Caravan. He felt terrible about that because if he had noticed Kevin a minute earlier, it might have made a difference. Ironically, Kevin used his first Aikido belt to tie himself to the support rail of the roll-up garage door.

While the fire department and paramedics were working on Kevin, the police told us they had received a phone call from Kelcey in Tucson who saw Kevin's post on Facebook. She knew he lived in Chandler and she called the police right away. First, the police went to Kevin's old apartment because that was the address they had on file for him. He wasn't there, so they looked at utility records to see if there was another Tejan in the area. That was us, and that's how they ended up knocking on our door.

Now the police said that we needed to hurry and get to the hospital right away. They were taking Kevin there. By the sound of that, we thought he might be ok. I asked if they got him breathing and they said "No." It was very confusing, but we hurried into our car and went to the hospital. We called my dad and stepmom while driving there to tell them what has happened. They said to call them as soon as we found out something more. My dad told me later that Barbara, my stepmom, just cried softly all night long after that phone call and into the early hours of the morning for Kevin and what had happened to him. She had lost her son to a gunshot wound years earlier and knew quite personally how deeply it hurt, and how devastating it was to the entire family.

As soon as we arrived at the hospital, they escorted us down the hall to a room and were asked to wait until the doctor came to talk with us. They said they were working on Kevin. We were still hopeful that he was going to be alright. Then the doctor came into the room along with the social worker. The doctor said they weren't able to save him. Our son was gone forever.

I don't think that information registered initially; it was just so hard to really believe. My eyes welled up with tears, but I wasn't able to completely cry until later. I remember repeating the events of the evening to the doctor and social worker and couldn't believe that it ended up this way. The social worker said she remembered us visiting several times when Kevin had attempted suicide other times. She said that she knew Kevin had been on a difficult path for a long time and knew that we were always there for him to support him and said that we were good parents to him. That was very nice to hear from her, and though we don't remember her being there, she remembered both of us.

I asked to see Kevin. I just wanted to be with him. They said they could take us to see him, and Paul held my hand as we walked down the long hospital hallway toward the room Kevin was in. I wanted to run down the hallway to him, but I didn't. I just felt like I couldn't get to him fast enough. I knew he was gone, but I wanted to be with him. We entered the room, and there he was, lying on a gurney bed. I remember that it looked narrow; hard and uncomfortable. Even though Kevin didn't look good when we saw him, at the same time, I couldn't take my eyes off of him. I just wanted to be there with him for every moment I could. I don't know why I felt ok looking at him, but that's what I did. Maybe I was trying to reason in my mind if it was all for real.

I'll never forget the look on Kevin's face as he laid there with a plastic tube sticking out of his mouth, and his eyes were fixed and turned to the right. I stroked his face and touched him and kissed his cheek. I just stood there looking at him. My baby was gone. It was a shock beyond words. Paul, on the other hand, looked at Kevin and then turned his head away for a moment. He couldn't believe that Kevin had done it this time. He had really killed himself.

Paul thought we had been there long enough, and he turned me away from Kevin to step outside the curtain. We both just stood there not knowing what to do. There was the hustle of doctors around us, and someone noticed us just standing there. They said to another person "Those are the parents of the young man in that room." Then they spoke to us and said they were waiting to hear from the ME. I asked, what is the ME? The medical examiner. Kevin would be transported downtown to the medical examiner's office for examination. Now when I hear ME on the television, I flash back to that moment when Kevin died.

Then the doctor and social worker led us back to the room where we were previously waiting. I didn't want to leave Kevin. It felt like such a short time spent with him, and although I knew there wasn't anything I could do, I just wanted to stay with him. Then a police officer came into the room to ask us questions. He said that he would be the officer to investigate what happened and needed to write a final report. The social workers were there also and were saying how they remembered Kevin from past suicide attempts. They confirmed that he had struggled a lot and was very depressed, and they remember us visiting Kevin and always being there to help him. The officer said he needed to go back to our house so he could complete his report, and there were other officers who needed to complete their investigation too, and they were waiting for us to return to the house. We had no idea that they were still at our house waiting for us to return.

Paul and I got in the car and drove back to our house so that we could meet the officers there. It was a very quiet drive home. It was heavy, and still. We kept going over the events of the evening with each other; sorting out what happened, trying to absorb everything as best we could in the moment. It was so disturbing, and we were entirely shocked that it had actually happened. Paul and I had discussed in the past that Kevin might actually commit suicide, but that was totally different from having to deal with it as it actually happened. It felt so wrong and shouldn't have happened. Our conversation that night has become a blur in my memory, hearing words we spoke aloud, but not sure whether they came from myself or from Paul. We said to each other, we knew he was very upset that night, and we should have known to watch him better, and know that something was "up" with him when he calmed down so fast after getting his computer up and running. We talked on and on about how we might have been able to change the events of the evening. Maybe Kevin had resolved things in his mind that tonight was the night he would succeed in his attempt. Maybe that's why he was calm and was checking when we would be going to bed for the evening.

When we arrived home, and the officer asked us to remain outside the house while he looked around to complete his investigation. All the while we were watching the forensic unit begin taking evidence and placing it in a bag and measuring things in the garage and taking photos to complete their report. We waited on the sidewalk in front of the house and watched while they did their work. There was yellow tape around our house while this was going on. The police officer who was to finalize the investigation of the case came out to talk to us. He said that Kevin had left a couple of suicide notes and they weren't very flattering to his dad and asked if we wanted him to delete the one on the computer. We said, "no." We'd been through a lot with Kevin, and there probably wasn't much that we hadn't heard already. He said that was ok and said he would not delete it. Kevin also wrote an unflattering note in a notebook that the police found in his room along with a bent closet door clothing rod. It appeared that Kevin had a test run using his bedroom closet to attempt suicide there earlier that evening. I remembered that as I was sitting in my bedroom, I had seen Kevin down the hall in his room. His door was open, and I heard this loud crashing sound. I asked him, "What was that?" He said, "Oh, I was just trying to put up something in my closet, and it fell." I didn't think anything more about it. Then he left his bedroom and went into the kitchen and got on the computer. Nothing appeared unusual at that point in the evening.

The police completed their investigation and left the house around 2:30 am. We let our dogs back into the house. They were unusually quiet, due to having strangers in the house moving around, but they must have known that something was wrong. Animals can be so sensitive to their surroundings. Paul and I were just sick to our stomachs. Did this just happen? My head was pounding; *This isn't happening, this isn't real. Oh God why. Why-why. This isn't happening.* My thoughts spun like a broken record spinning a million miles an hour, all while repeating the same questions in my head, questions I did not have the answer to. Questions I just didn't want to answer at all. I wanted to throw up. I couldn't sleep. I just cried. I cried myself to sleep for a short time and still felt sick when I woke up.

I kept wishing it was just a bad dream. I wanted this to go away; I wanted the pain to stop. For a moment I would say to myself, *maybe it didn't happen.* I wanted so badly to wake up, and see Kevin breathing and playing on the computer, and not think about where he was at that moment.

What was next? What would we do now? I felt so lost and sad, and lonely, and was trying to sort it out, but my thoughts were like a tangled ball of yarn a million miles long, and I was trying in vain to sort it all out. I just wanted this sick feeling in my stomach to go away, to curl up in a corner and die. I just wanted Kevin back. Feeling all of this was almost unbearable. Paul and I kept repeating the events of the previous evening, as if in some way we could make sense of it all, as if we would find the answer we'd been searching for since Kevin began struggling so many years earlier. Maybe it's a way the mind attempts to come to grips with what really happened, a way to let your mind accept that it *did* happen.

Paul said, "Let's go drive somewhere and get something to eat so we don't feel any sicker than we do." We ended up at restaurant we hadn't ever gone to before. It took all of our energy to drag ourselves into the restaurant and eat a few bites of a meal that we shared. We were so miserable.

I remember calling my Mom that morning and having to tell her that her only grandchild had committed suicide. She just cried. She could hardly believe what I was saying. Kevin and my Mom were very close and had that special grandmother and grandson bond. It was very hard on her to hear of Kevin's passing.

PART FOUR: THERE WILL BE HOPE

COPING WITH LOSS

Life isn't easy, and the ups and downs that come with living with a child with a spectrum disorder and various degrees of mental illness are very challenging. It's a lot of work, but well worth the effort. Even going through all of the heartache we have endured, I wouldn't change my decision in wanting to have a child. You never know what you're going to get when you conceive naturally or by some medical intervention. The best you can do is love and value your child and family and give the best of yourself, and hope for a bright future.

How do you cope with the loss of a loved one? Many might say "Not very well at times," and I'd also like to say to those people, "That's o.k." Losing a child feels like a living hell. It hurts for a long time, and the pain never goes away completely. There is a continual knowing that he was there and now he is gone forever.

Our busy life together was our norm. We were either going to the grocery store, the mall, or a home improvement store, going to school or work, Taekwondo practice, the movies, hunting down beanie babies or new magic tricks, driving to grandma or grandpa's house. Then we had thrown into the mix a few angry outbursts, obsessive-compulsive meltdowns, teacher's meetings, doctors' appointments, and trips to the hospital, and there you have it...a normal family life, filled with lots of activities. We figured it was normal for families to go through this type of chaos and just keep "keeping on" every day. We knew life was extreme at times, and all families didn't have to be concerned with an anger outburst, or an emotional breakdown, or visits to the psychiatrist, but we thought we coped pretty well. Every family has their own type of struggles and issues to deal with, it's just a part of life; and yes, it puts a stress and strain on anyone's life. It's all in how you respond to a situation, and learn from it, and move forward from it that shapes your future, one day at a time. There isn't any easy road or magic pill that helps you bounce back to your previous life filled with carefree thoughts, no burdens or worries to get you down.

When Kevin died, we looked back on what we had gone through as a family and realized that many days weren't like other families. We had been through a lot of extreme life situations that I wouldn't wish anyone to have to experience, but of course, there are many families who can relate and have experienced these difficult times. Life shouldn't have to be so hard. Our house is so much quieter now. It feels very empty at times, like my thoughts echo against the open spaces that used to be filled with Kevin and his energy, in all of its varying degrees. I look around and imagine when he walked through the door and went straight to the pantry for a snack or soda, or was in his room on his computer, or taking walks with his dad and I and the dogs.

His Dad and I would go out to eat, and we would sit and talk about Kevin and reminisce about both the good times and bad. We were frustrated that we couldn't turn things around, they kept going from bad to worse and more frequently. With all of the different doctors and treatments, he went through, you would have thought more could have been accomplished. When we see other children at the mall, or grocery store, or see them on television shows, we notice how different many of them act compared to how Kevin did. We notice their giddiness and animated expressions, or how they act when playing with their toys or talking with the other kids on the playground. Kevin was so much more withdrawn as a child and didn't show much enthusiasm or run around and act silly like many other children do.

I thought it was great that Paul and I shared these feelings and memories with each other. I know it has helped both of us move through the stages of grief and to cope with losing Kevin. People would ask if we were going to sell our house and move elsewhere because of all the memories there, but we never felt the need to move. To us, everywhere we drove, we pass by places where we have memories of doing things with Kevin. It's not something that can easily be escaped. Yes, it's sad, and I cry at times; however, it was our opportunity for Paul and me to talk about our feelings and "remember when" this and that happened. Everyone is different and deals with tragedies in their own way. However, that looks. This is just how it has looked for us.

Paul and I talked about how Obsessive-Compulsive Disorder can be deadly. When applying it to Kevin's situation, we now see how OCD was the underlying force that always pushed him to the next level, which wasn't a good thing. Kevin was first consumed by his online game he played, and then he was obsessed over his physical appearance after losing so much weight that it pushed him to the other side of not wanting to eat at all and then purging what he did eat. It bothered him that the doctors didn't think his case was serious enough to get him help. The doctors didn't value his feelings; they just medicated him. He was so intensely focused on what was important to him at the time. He couldn't ever see the big picture. There are those who obsess over touching something numerous times, doing things in a certain order, turning on and off a light switch over and over again. So many ways that one can get stuck in their brain, like focusing too much on a particular subject that it just eats away at one's self-confidence, self-esteem, and overall life. It's that serious. It's not a joke to make fun of someone for acting out that way. It's an obsessive behavior that becomes so negative and destructive in your life that you can't think of anything else, but to end it all.

Paul and I firmly believe that if Kevin wasn't so obsessed with whatever he was focused on at the time, he would be here with us today. Yes, depression and other mental health problems are extremely serious; however, if you couple it with Obsessive Compulsive Disorder, it's a recipe for disaster, and a deadly combination of disorders is created. The mind is a beautiful thing and can also be as destructive as it is beautiful, delicate as it is strong.

DREAMS

Most nights following Kevin's death, I would cry myself to sleep, say a prayer and ask God for strength to get through this painful time, and try to find something positive each day to begin healing my heart and soul. The nights were the worst for me. Trying to fall asleep felt impossible, and the only thing I could think of was Kevin. I missed him so much and was so sad he was gone. He left me, and I was kind of mad at him. I knew his life was difficult, but his dad and I always told him that the doctors were always developing new medicines, new treatments and learning more and more about our DNA that could bring forth answers and solutions to why some suffer from these mental illnesses. I wish he could have held on longer.

Shortly after he died, I began having a lot of very vivid dreams and experiencing other events that were not of this world. It's as if Kevin was checking on me, making sure I was o.k. It's no wonder because he was constantly on my mind. Many of the dreams were not normal dreams where you wake up in the morning, and you can't remember all the details. I had those dreams also, but when I had a very vivid one, I would write it down, and I began dating them after a while. I'm so glad I did this. Looking back and reading what I dreamt brings all of those feelings back of when I had them, and how fantastic I felt that next day because I felt so connected to Kevin again. The dreams weren't scary at all; they were very comforting. I have also smelled different smells when not expecting it and have also seen Kevin standing on the side of the road. Paul saw him too at the same time. No, I'm not crazy. It was very strange and hard to believe, but very real. I'm really glad I've experienced these strange phenomenons. I'd like to share some of my dreams and experiences because I think it has been a significant part of my healing process and trying to move forward after a horrible event.

My first vivid dream was seeing Kevin in a church pew behind me when I was at a women's conference with my longtime friend, Belinda. I turned around and said to him, "What are you doing here? This is a women's conference." He just looked at me and smiled and appeared very happy. I was on cloud nine the next morning. It was so real, and Kevin seemed very content, and that made me happy.

Another time I dreamed he was in a grocery store just sitting on the floor reading a book. He was around age twenty-five this time.

One time I experienced what I would call an "event" as I'm not sure what else to call it: One day while getting ready for work, I opened my jewelry box to put on my jewelry for the day and smelled this very fragrant scent coming from it. I had never noticed it all the other days I had opened my jewelry box. It smelled like an old ladies' perfume and mothballs. I laughed and identified it with Kevin at that moment. I did have a lock of his hair in an envelope in my jewelry box, and it smelled fragrant too.

Paul has also had dreams about Kevin, and one night he dreamt that he and Kevin were sitting on a bench eating a big bowl of raspberries together, something they both had shared a love for. It was very vivid, and it made Paul smile that day.

11/28/2013 - Thanksgiving Day dream - I was at my mom's house, and there was both living relatives and those who had passed away in the same room, along with Paul and my dad. Kevin had school the next day but forgot his school backpack and brought his little green suitcase instead, which contained his toys. Somehow, I had to fit his suitcase into mine because I was flying to Las Vegas the next morning for a job interview and had to get him to school also. My dad was taking the car and driving to his meeting in San Diego. I'm not sure how everyone was going to get to where they needed to go. My cousin, Julie, was complimenting her mom on her white crochet sweater and she said oh I wore this old sweater when I was pregnant with you, and they hugged. What I find strange is there was a mix of the living and others who had passed on already in my dream, and some had never met each other, but we were all in the same room intertwined. It was an interesting dream.

Another event on 12/20/2013 - I was sitting at the computer in our bedroom and felt a tap on my back. I turned around, and no one was there. Paul was sitting on the bed, not anywhere near me. I immediately thought of Kevin. I wasn't afraid. It feels strange when it happens, the thought of Kevin pops into my head, and I associate it with him. I don't know for sure, but at the time it felt like he was there to say hello.

Here's another event - 01/16/2014 - I was in bed trying to fall asleep. I was thinking of Kevin and how much I missed him. I felt a light kiss on my left cheek. It was comforting, and I stopped crying and was able to fall asleep.

02/05/2104 - I dreamed we were at a lake somewhere. Someone asked me where was Kevin? I said over there, and there came Kevin with two other friends just getting out of the water. They had been swimming together and were smiling and having fun. Kevin looked like a teenager.

02/08/2014 - This time my dream included Heather. I was taking a test on a laptop and failed the test because I was counting wrong and was recording the wrong answer even though I knew the correct answer. I left the testing area and came back later to finish, but this time I was carrying an infant girl. She was only a few days old and was sleeping nicely all wrapped up in a tight blanket. I answered another few questions and left without finishing the test at some employment center. I came back again to finish the test, but this time Paul was with me. I signed him into the testing area, along with Heather, and I signed in to finish the test. This time she woke up and looked so pretty. It was hard taking the test, juggling the laptop and watching her. Someone in the room said he had looked at her heart and he was going to get her some medicine that would make it stronger. He said she looked weak. Before I woke up, I remember telling her I would be a better mother tomorrow. It was the first time I remember dreaming that I was holding Heather. It felt wonderful.

02/14/2014 - I dreamed Kevin was around two years old and Grandma Neubauer (my mom) called him over to her to ride on the merry-go-round. You know the type of rides that are outside the grocery store; the ones that you put in a quarter in and it goes around for a few minutes? Kevin loved those. They had fun together. It was many years ago where these rides were placed outside the grocery stores, but I don't recall seeing them anymore.

04/30/2014 - Around 3:30 a.m. the computer in our bedroom came on by itself. I figured a dog bumped it, but no dog around anywhere. I got up to put it back to sleep and went back to bed. While trying to fall back asleep, I heard musical notes at a high pitch in my left ear. It was a pretty tune. I associated it was Kevin coming to check in on me and say "hi." I felt his presence, and it was very comforting to me.

07/08/2014 - I dreamed Kevin got a new game and he wanted to show it to me. He said I had to guess which item he was thinking of. He had set up lots of objects and toys under his bed. I crawled on my knees and looked under the bed. I chose something, can't remember what it was, and Kevin said no that's not it, and I said yes, it is. I had guessed it, and he couldn't believe it. It's only because I was watching his face when I was looking at different objects and read is facial cues. He was young, about six years old.

07/20/2014 - We were on a bus going to camp. It was a crowded city bus, and the bus driver was telling this long story that everyone on the bus was interested to hear. Now it was our time to get off the bus because we had arrived at our camp that was near a lake. Paul helped get the boat into the water. I walked right by a black bear and petted it and said: "Hi nice bear." Then the camp leader said "Hi" to us and said, "So this must be Kevin." Shook his hand and said, "Nice to meet you, Kevin." I was holding him in my arms, and Kevin was around three or four years old at the time. Then the alarm clock went off.

08/25/2014 - I dreamed Kevin and my mom were holding hands and skipping and laughing. This time I was sad when I woke up from the dream because I knew it would be true that when my mom does die, she would be with Kevin holding hands, skipping, and laughing and I wouldn't be. They would watch out for each other so that part would be good, but I would be missing both of them so deeply. This dream was especially hard for me all week-long thinking about the fact that my mom would most likely be joining Kevin sooner than I would be, and that I would miss them both so very much.

This next dream is from one of Kevin's friends, Zady. She was extremely affected when she learned of Kevin's passing. She and I talk once in a while, and she called me this day to tell me about a dream she had about Kevin the previous night. She said it felt so real like it wasn't a dream at all –

08/31/2014 - Zady dreamed that she and Kevin were walking down the street, away from Starr (a day program they both attended) to the area where they hung out. Kevin said to Zady to tell my mom and dad that he loved them and missed them and to not cry that he wasn't there. He was o.k. He also told Zady that he missed talking to her and that he loved her too. He also said that Emmalee, her daughter, was getting so big (he has never met Emmalee). Then he said he had a message for her to give to Adam, her husband. Zady said "why don't you just tell him yourself," and Kevin said he couldn't get to Adam. He said, "that Adam better be very good to her and if he wasn't, when Adam died, Kevin was going to kick his butt." Kevin also told Zady that when she died, she was to meet Kevin at their special place. It was down the street from Starr in between the buildings where they hung out. He would meet up with her there. He also said that he was always with us and always around us.

10/07/2014 - It was hard waking up this morning. I kept hitting the sleep button, then I rolled over towards Paul and was falling back asleep again went I heard Kevin say "Mom." I woke up right away and looked toward our doorway where Kevin had stood before. It sounded just like him, and I felt he was there with me. He was saying it was time to get up or I would be late for work.

10/15/2014 - Just before waking up this morning on my birthday, I saw a newborn baby boy with a blue knit cap on his head. It was so clear and made me feel happy inside. I'm interpreting the event as Kevin saying Happy Birthday, Mom.

10/18/2014 – Paul and I were visiting my dad and stepmom's house and were gathering up our things to go home. Kevin was in the middle of the room dancing around. His Grandma Barbara was taking pictures of Kevin. I walked over to my Dad and said "Kevin looks good. It's like he's really here with us." I looked back to where he was dancing, and he was gone.

11/25/2014 - I dreamed that my mom and I went to a magic show to watch this particular magician perform. We were sitting on the balcony watching the children crowding around the front of the stage waiting for the magician to begin his show. They all wanted to show the magician what magic tricks they could also do. Kids ran to meet the magician at the right side of the stage, but Kevin and his friend went to the left side of the stage. Kevin was trying to be the first on stage to show the other magician what he could do too. His friend was right behind him. Kevin got to the stage first, and his friend yelled to Kevin "Get the microphone!" Kevin stumbled and grabbed the mic. Somehow his shirt got tangled with the mic cord, and he got very frustrated and began tearing off his shirt. Everyone loved it. The crowd was cheering. Kevin flexed his well-developed muscles and started his performance. He looked great!

12/19/2014 - When lying in bed trying to make myself get up for the day, there were hundreds of twinkling lights above, right at the ceiling fan. They were gold, and only where the fan was. Maybe it was Kevin saying good morning and those were all of his friends with him. It made me smile, and ready to get up out of bed.

12/24/2014 - When I was just about to wake up this morning, I saw a baby wrapped up tightly in a blanket. He was sleeping. I thought it might be Kevin saying hello.

09/12/2015 - It has been awhile since I had a vivid dream about Kevin. This night I dreamed that Paul was sitting in a chair, and Kevin was sitting on him leaning back on his chest. He was around eight or nine years old. I spoke to him and told him how much I missed him, and I touched his face and neck and chest and said to him "You feel so real like you are sitting there." I put my forehead to his forehead and said: "I wish you were still with me." He said, "I know, but I'm here now."

This wasn't a dream, but a very strange event that happened to both Paul and I at the same time, while very much awake.

02/08/2016 - We just got home from work, and I sat down on the couch with our dog, Spike. There wasn't anything unusual about that. Then I went to prepare dinner, and Paul sat on the couch where Spike and I had been sitting. All of a sudden Paul said eeuw, yuck. It smells like fish. I was just over on the couch, and I didn't smell anything. Then I walked over to the couch, and I smelled it too. It was a very strong smell like Kimchi. I said maybe it was Kevin visiting and saying "hi." He loved Kimchi, and he knew that we couldn't stand the smell. It smelled so bad that we wouldn't allow him to open up the jar inside the house. If he wanted to eat Kimchi, he had to take it outside, eat it outside, close up the container before bringing it back in and placing it in the refrigerator. It was fermented vegetables. It reminded me of the Asian grocery store where he would buy it. Sometimes I think he did it just to make us mad. The store smelled like they mopped their floors with nasty, roly-poly fish heads. He thought it was funny that we didn't like going there because the smell would knock you over when you walked in the front door. Once you got over the smell, it was a very interesting international grocery store with some good prices, too.

That evening, if Kevin wanted to make an impression and come say "hi" to us, he certainly did that. It had to have been from his influence. What else could it be? It smelled so bad and was so real. We cleaned under the couch looking for a source of the smell like maybe something died there. There were only dust bunnies and dog hair clippings. The leather couch got cleaned extremely well that night, and everything smelled just fine afterward. That was so bizarre.

This is another dream from one of Kevin's friends, Zady. Kevin was her best friend. She called me today to tell me of a very vivid dream she had about him. She calls it one of those "visitation" types of dreams where it is so clear and vivid, and it gives one a feeling of peace and happiness later.

06/10/2016 - Zady dreamt she was in a very bright white area like a hospital. This man said to her, Room 48. He's in Room 48. She goes to Room 48, and there is Kevin standing in a very bright white room wearing a white dress shirt and white tuxedo type pants with white shoes. He said "Hi Zady, what are you doing here? How are you doing?" Then he looks at his watch and looks back at her. He did this three times. Then he said, "it's not your time, you have to go back. I love you, but it's not your time." Then he poked her, and she woke up. She said it felt so real and that she felt happy all day long from her dream. I told her that sounded like a nice dream.

What I didn't tell her was that I was looking at our monthly Homeowners Association receipt a few days prior and happened to notice that we lived on Lot 48. Something I hadn't thought of in many years since we bought our house. Then when she had that dream, it felt like some connection from Kevin through Zady to me. I might be over stretching here since it was her dream and not mine, but it was a nice dream for her.

This event touched both Paul and I as we carpooled to work each day.

06/13/2016 – Most of the time we turn up Rural Rd. and drive through a school zone which is 35 mph. Today we were stopped at the light, right in front of the high school, and we both noticed a young man standing near the wall of the school. Paul noticed that he was standing awkward. Paul mentioned it, and I agreed with him. We both thought he looked like Kevin. We kept staring and as we drove by we had to turn our heads 180 degrees to keep looking at him. It was incredible how much he looked like Kevin. His hair, his stature, his face! I'm glad Paul noticed it also, otherwise he would have just thought it was one of my crazy thoughts and visions I have every once in a while. It brought great happiness to me this morning. I kept saying to myself "I saw Kevin." It was a good start to a Monday morning.

Almost five years have now passed since Kevin passed away. I can't believe it has been that long. I am still so heartbroken and want to hold him close to me, so badly. I wish Kevin would just walk through the front door and say, "I'm home" as if nothing had happened. I understand all too well that this will never be possible, but the truth of how I feel and deal with losing him is mine to feel the way I want to feel.

HELLO, GRIEF

How does one heal after going through an extreme tragedy? Can healing be accomplished? Will life ever feel normal again? These are questions that have run through my mind, and I would guess that I'm not alone in that.

We won't know how much we can heal if we don't try. It's about making deliberate, daily, sometimes hourly choices, making an effort every day to think positive thoughts, giving yourself grace for the negative ones, and keeping the lines of honest communication open with your support system. My support system is God, my husband, my family, friends, and coworkers. Everyone has been so loving and caring for what Paul and I have gone through these past five years. It's difficult for people to imagine how awful it is unless they have experienced it themselves. Any loss is a difficult loss, and I've been told that losing a child is even more traumatic. I would agree with that. When a spouse dies, or when a child loses their parents, we have words to describe that; widowed, an orphan. There is no word, however, for a parent who has lost a child. I don't want others to feel uncomfortable around me, knowing that we have lost both of our children and them not knowing what to say. I want to be approachable by others and be available to help my friends, family, and strangers if they ever have need. It's been therapeutic writing out my thoughts and memories, both the good and the bad ones. They are all memories that make us who we are today. These memories make me laugh and cry; they bring me joy, sadness, confusion and frustration, anger and hurt, and most of all love and forgiveness. Grief is not linear. In those immediate moments of trauma, it can feel like I'm standing amidst a devastating earthquake, but what no one ever tells you is that there are those sneaky aftershocks that hit without warning. You never know when a "sad" feeling will hit you. I choose life over death, and I have a lot more to accomplish in my lifetime. Some days I will feel as though I have made a certain progress. On others, I feel those aftershocks hit, and I just have to allow the hurt to roll over me and experience it. I know despite it all, that it will pass; I truly believe that no matter what, there is hope ahead.

TRYING TO MOVE FORWARD
AFTER A TRAGEDY

After we lost Kevin, we tried keeping ourselves busy. Paul took on a lot of house projects like staining a new cabinet for the kitchen and installing solar panels on our house. I joined Toastmasters and put more energy into writing this book. We did some gardening and installed wood laminate floors.

We also visited a medium named Mary Martin, who was instrumental in bringing some light back into my sad soul. She mentioned that rose quartz was a stone with healing properties, so I decided to buy some the next time I went through Quartzite. I have a large piece of rose quartz by my bedside, and a little heart shaped stone in my desk at work. I'll take it out of my desk once in a while, and it makes me smile. I don't notice anything in particular as far as the healing properties, but it's a very pretty stone. Mary had her "Barbie" doll (a vessel used to allow others to come and use her) sitting next to her. Kevin was there and spoke to us through her. Mary's voice sounded different when she was talking, but she didn't sound like Kevin. Some of her demeanor was definitely like Kevin. It was very purposeful in trying to get his point across to us. He wanted us to know that he has forgiven himself and God has forgiven him. He was sick and didn't feel good in his mind. He couldn't control it and wanted it to go away and was tired of fighting it. Mary asked if there was a note left behind, and we said yes. He said those things he wrote in the note were hurtful, and he didn't mean them. He wanted for us to wash the words away like water blurring them out.

Then Mary turned to me, she knelt down and took my hand and said it was Kevin holding my hand. He said in a very strong way that it was not my fault. Nothing was my fault. You did nothing wrong.

So now Kevin knows about why I couldn't get pregnant and that the eggs he developed from had been stolen and not given freely. He said he was now "aware" of it all and would make it right. He has been waiting for us to all meet altogether. He wanted to meet. It was an incredible feeling we both had after she spoke with us through this "vessel" she used to communicate.

After meeting with Mary, I felt so much better about dealing with Kevin's loss, and for the next couple of days, I was in a remarkably good and upbeat mood. Paul was also amazed with some of her discoveries and comments that day. I know that she helped to make some sense of my intense sadness over losing Kevin. It didn't hurt as much when I would be in a store somewhere and see other babies or young children. There were times when I would feel so emotional, and many times I would cry. They reminded me of how much I missed my children, and the sadness was very intense. It was like a turning point in my healing process that allowed me to cope with things a little better. All in all, I felt better after meeting with her. Whether it was real or not, I know I benefited from the experience.

WHERE HAVE ALL THE CHILDREN GONE?

Ever since Kevin was seven years old and we discovered that the donated eggs in which he and his sister became living souls, weren't donated at all, but taken without the knowledge of the donor mom (Christina Marie), I've thought about her so many times through the years. What a nightmare she had to endure, just like us. How was she doing? Where was she now? I wish she could have met Kevin and had a part in his life. Now that he is gone I feel so bad that she never met him while he was alive. I wanted to write her and tell her what happened.

It was October 2013, six months after Kevin died. Thanksgiving and Christmas were right around the corner. I didn't want to ruin her holiday, so I waited to write her. January came, and it still weighed heavily on my mind. I had to tell her. His birthday was the next month, and he would have turned 26. I called the Orange County Register and emailed them trying to locate anyone who could get a letter to her. No one would respond to me. It had been so long that all of the original reporters on the story had moved on or retired. Twenty years is a long time. When I reached out to the attorney's office, I ran into a brick wall there also. The attorney emailed me back and said that she wasn't his client and he couldn't help. I was at a loss of what to do at this point.

I wondered about the other approximately one hundred children who were born from eggs that weren't given consensually but stolen. Where were they now? Has anyone reached out to try and connect with the biological mothers or have any mothers reached out to their biological children? I've always wondered about that. They would be adults now, between twenty and thirty years old. My prayer for them is that they are healthy and happy and find joy in living, wherever they are.

Where is Dr. Asch? He surely affected many families; in a good way for those of us who were lucky enough to achieve pregnancy and the birth of a child. At the same time, however, he destroyed lives in other cases where their eggs were stolen and resulted in children born to couples the donors will never know. He created an earthquake of unsettled lives in so many families. He may have thought he was doing everyone a favor but didn't think about the consequences if his secret got out. That was very selfish of him and any other participants in this charade. There were some parents who did find out where their eggs ended up and had to watch from a distance their children grow up, being raised by other families, as the biological parents were cut out of the children's lives. In any of these situations, it's very tragic and shouldn't have ever happened. I've always wondered what his motivation might have been to do something like this to so many people. Was it money, prestige, power? Or was there a larger organization pulling strings for profit, making him do things he might not have done if they weren't funding his fertility center and research? We may never know the answers to these questions. What I do know is there has to be honesty and truthfulness in the infertility world when dealing with the most personal part of a woman's body – reproductive life.

THREE YEARS LATER

It's December 2016, three and a half years later since losing him, and this year has been the hardest. I'm more emotional, depressed, and frustrated thinking that this is the way it is and I just have to get used to it. Kevin is gone, and nothing can change that. Death is forever. Our Christmas this year is centered around the dogs. We bought them stuffed animals, and I even wrapped them up. Kind of silly, but they are the kids now. I didn't feel like putting up a tree. I had the two years previously, but this year, it just made me so sad to think about putting up the ornaments that Kevin made in school and special ones I had saved through the years. Paul put lights outside on the house, and I hung a wreath on the door. That was it. We will also be alone this Christmas as family is going other places this year. I just feel like we aren't wanted. I know that's not true, but it's a little tougher this year trying to be happy about the holidays.

Feelings of despair, sadness, loneliness are all prevalent. I sure hope I snap out of this soon. I wish I had more vivid dreams like in the past. They sure cheered me up. I dreamed last night when he was around seven or eight, and we were shopping. Not much detail, but I remember how he was such a cute little guy. He always made me smile.

I wish Kevin would walk through the door, smile, and say, "Mom, do you want to see a magic trick?"

EPILOGUE

It's March 2017, and I've been thinking a lot about needing to finish this book. I don't know why I feel so compelled to focus on it and get it done. I look around sometimes and still feel Kevin's presence. I know he is gone, but at times I'll be planning a meal or driving down a street or watching a movie and I think that Kevin would like that for dinner or that movie on TV would be a movie Kevin would enjoy. Then I say to myself, *he's not here*, but I still want to include him in my thoughts. I don't want to forget him; what he liked, how he acted and him just being around making me smile. I wonder how long I'll have these feelings and thoughts. We were close and created many memories, the good and bad ones. Life sure wasn't boring with Kevin. With Heather, I only have a few memories which I'll treasure forever; however, she isn't in my thoughts every day like Kevin is. I feel a little guilty about that; she pops into my mind once in a while, or I'll have a dream every several years, and every birthday and the day she died is always on my mind. Those days are still difficult to get through. She was the beginning, and Kevin was the end. I feel that I'm not a mother some days. I lost both my children. Then I have to count my blessings and be thankful for the time I had with them both. There are some out there who have never experienced motherhood, and I am thankful that God granted me that special time in my life.

As I was writing this book, I was going through the newspaper articles about the fertility scandal and came across an article that sounded like it matched my situation, and the woman's name was in the article. I looked her up on the internet, and a lot about her matched what I already knew, as well as the area she lived in and her profession. The pieces of the puzzle seem to fit. I looked up her Facebook site and gasped. She looked similar to me. The nurses said that they were pleased that the donor match was really good and she looked like we could be sisters. Could this be the donor mom, that I now refer to as Christina Marie? Now I feel guilty that if it's her; her name has been in my book of articles for over twenty years. I had always wanted to reach out to her but was told it wouldn't benefit Kevin. So, we didn't. Now I ask myself, should we reach out now, and see if it is her? How will she feel if it is her, with Kevin gone, knowing she will never meet him? I think she would experience all the pain that Paul and I have processed for five years now. I'm not sure if we should open her up to that.

On the other hand, as a mother, I would be thinking about learning that there was a child out there who was part of me, and now he would be almost thirty years old, and the other parents (us) haven't contacted her like we said we would many years ago, and I want to make the right decision. I don't want anyone to experience added hurt. I hope she is healthy and happy.

She was so extremely important to Paul and I many years ago, and she didn't even know how greatly she impacted our lives. I'm grateful that I had Paul, Kevin's father, and we still do have each other today. We have gone through so much with Kevin from the beginning to the end. I can't even imagine doing it without Paul's help. We depended on one another so much as Kevin was growing up, and we sure needed each other to help get Kevin all raised up. We did the very best that we knew how to do. I just wish the outcome was different, but one thing I have learned is this: You can't live your life fearing the loss of your child. Life isn't meant to be that way.

Lightning can strike out of no-where on a clear blue-sky day, and the darkness can seem to last forever, but there is hope for us all, and light in even the very blackest of tunnels. All lives are fragile and are to be respected, loved and appreciated for all that God has given us.

-The End-

March 7, 1988

To my very first grandchild,

I'm writing to you today my dearest baby Kevin, to give you just a glimpse of how very special you are. You will never know the many lives that your birth has touched and I was afraid we might forget some of it if I didn't write it down for you.

Your mother called me about noon on February 13, 1988 and said you would be born that day. She was crying because it really was too soon for you to enter this big, hard world. You hadn't had time to gain enough weight. But...at 4:41 p.m. here you were – a big 1 lb. 15 oz. boy, 13 inches long, with black hair on a tiny little head. You were the tiniest, cutest little baby any of us had ever seen.

Your Dad rushed out and bought a balloon to hand above your bed which said on it, "You're So Special". Those words couldn't have said it any better for the way your parents felt about you, your Uncle Larry, or your grandparents who were all there to welcome you with much joy and excitement.

As life began for you in that tiny little bed at Loma Linda University Hospital, your family, friends, and strangers all over California were praying that God would help you make it through each day. People were calling every day to ask how baby Kevin was doing. We wanted so much for you to gain weight and grow strong so you could come home.

Your Mommy and Daddy visited you every day. They took pictures of you every time you moved and did everything they could to make your stay in the hospital comfortable while you were away from them.

The first few weeks I came to visit you (Grandparents could visit only once a week) it was so hard to just look at you, pat you and not be able to hold you. When we talked to you, you would squirm as if you were trying to wake up and please us. You opened your eyes a little and oh, what a thrill to see you do that.

Kevin, there are a lot of people in this world who have no idea if they were loved as a child, so I want you to have this letter to read when you grow up and to know that no baby could have been wanted more or loved more than you.

You are so special, my dearest little grandson.

Much love,

Grandma

NOTE TO READERS

I've poured out my heart, my soul, and my most personal feelings and thoughts about my life into this book, hoping that something good will come from it all. This book has been a lifetime in the making, and I hope and pray that others who are struggling with infertility, can know that their dreams can also come true. Every hormone shot, every ultrasound, and every blood test you have to go through are worth it in the end when you hold your child in your arms.

The procedures I went through are now ancient history, being thirty years ago. They were true miracles then, and it's amazing to see today how far advanced fertility treatments have come.

If you are contemplating a fertility procedure now, you are thirty years luckier than we were. I wish you all the best on your journey and challenge you to always think positively. Dream about that beautiful little face looking into your eyes, completely dependent upon you. As a new parent, you gaze back with your eyes filled with love, excitement, hopefulness, and a little fear of parenting this perfect little bundle; lives forever changed.

As I mentioned early on, you never know whether you will give birth to a healthy child or a child with developmental issues, or behavioral health issues. You get what you get and being a parent of a special needs child is a huge responsibility. A very special responsibility that calls for a lot of patience and determination to keep working towards a solution to whatever your child needs at that time. If your child is struggling with a spectrum disorder, know that there are support groups out there and new technologies that are discovered all the time. I just wish Kevin could have held on a little longer to try them out. Even though our story with Kevin ended, hope for those who struggle with similar battles didn't die with him. Hope is still there, and joy is still possible. Having open communication with your child is so important for the day when they decide to come to you to discuss a difficult subject. It will be a little easier for them to open up if you were always willing to listen to what they said in the past.

FAMILY THE HARD WAY